# THE RAILS AND SAILS
# OF WELSH SLATE

# The Rails and Sails
## of Welsh Slate

Alun John Richards

First published in 2011

© Alun John Richards

© Llygad Gwalch 2011

ISBN: 978-1-84524-174-2

Cover design: Lynwen Jones
Cover Images: *Front upper:* Ships at Aberdyfi
*Front lower:* Padarn Railway
Back Inserts: *Upper:* Porth Penrhyn, Bangor
*Middle:* Tal-y-cafn Ferry, Dyffryn Conwy
*Lower:* Rhiw-bach Tramway, Blaenau Ffestiniog
*Background:* Abercwmeiddaw, Upper Corris

Published by Llygad Gwalch,
Ysgubor Plas, Llwyndyrys,
Pwllheli, Gwynedd, Wales, LL53 6NG,

www.carreg-gwalch.com

*Dedicated to –*
*Griff Jones, Lewis Lloyd, Dafydd Price*
*and Merfyn Williams,*
*in whose shadows I was privileged to stand.*

*And remembering –*
*They that go down to the sea in ships, and occupy their*
*business in great waters.*

# Author's Preface

Much has been written in recent years about Welsh slate quarries and their total dominance of global production. Even more has been said about the railways that served that industry and were the model for narrow-gauge railways throughout the world, many of which are still with us as the 'Great Little Trains of Wales'. There have been a number of exceedingly well-researched works about the ships that traditionally carried the product to its destination and formed the greatest dedicated assemblage of ships since the Greeks sailed for Troy.

This book attempts to briefly co-ordinate these three elements and their evolvement not just into an industry but also into a proud tradition.

# Contents

# Introduction

Traditionally most British slate occurs in Wales, predominately in the more rugged, sparsely populated and hence poorer regions where it was not until at least the 17th century that there was much escape from a barter economy based on subsistence agriculture, the only roof being crude thatch. Therefore local demand was negligible.

Slate was used for Roman forts, Norman castles and for the richer religious institutions, only gradually filtering through to public buildings and the more prestigious private houses. Such slate roofs as were required would be erected by 'slaters' who laid slates they had made from rock that they themselves had dug from outcrops.

Although direct evidence of routes and destinations is sparse, by the 15th century it is clear that even the small tonnages produced in Wales exceeded local requirements, and hence distant markets were being found. By the 16th century landowners were seeing slate as an additional 'crop' to be won either by diggers paying a tribute or by their own men when farm work was slack. Although the annual quantities involved amounted to a mere hundred tons or so some was being sent to England and Ireland as well as other parts of Wales.

Growth continued during the 17th century and by the early 18th century annual tonnages had reached several thousand. However in these pre-canal, pre-railway days the cost of overland transport was prohibitive. Some producers in north-eastern Wales were able to reach the English Midlands by comparatively good roads but for the most part Welsh slate reached its markets by sea and production was largely confined to places close to the coast. Thus shipping, shipbuilding and seafaring became an integral part of the Welsh slate industry.

The real expansion in Welsh slate began in 1763 at the end of the Seven Years War. Europe settled into its modern form and the quarter century of peace that followed brought prosperity at home and export opportunities abroad. The development of shipping and a commercial infrastructure enabled Welsh slate digging to convert itself from a vernacular occupation to a bona fide industry.

Concomitant with the expansion of quarrying and of shipping was the problem of getting the product from quarry to ship which in almost road-less regions was usually by pack animals. Even where roads were available or could be built, the total cost of a load of slates delivered to say a Baltic port could comprise - one-third the cost of the slates ex-quarry, one-third the cost of the sea freight and one-third the cartage of maybe less than ten miles to a port.

From the beginning of the 19th century narrow gauge horse-gravity lines began to be laid, often reducing the cost of carriage by up to 90% and by the middle of that century the standard gauge main-line network came into the picture.

At the same time quarry settlements became towns, creeks became harbours, seaside villages became ports - and ships were built wherever a flat, water-adjacent piece of ground presented itself. All accompanied by a score or more of trades and professions that converted coast and hill into centres of skill-excellence.

Thus the whole edifice of the Welsh Slate Industry was a triptych of quarry, rails and shipping.

Although by the early 20th century the role of the local ports waned and motor lorries came into use, it was the 1960s before the last consignment of slate left a quarry by a narrow gauge line and the last load of roofing slate was loaded at a traditional slate port.

# Welsh Slate – The Maritime Connection

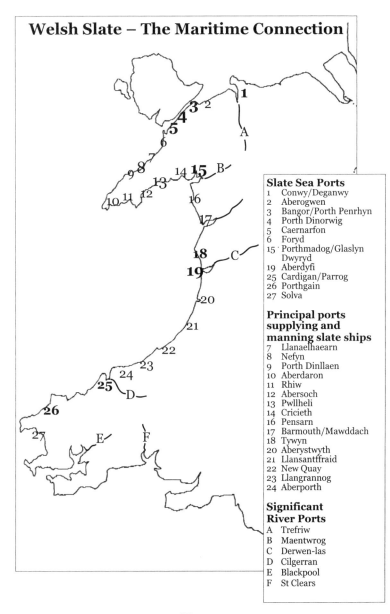

## Slate Sea Ports

1 Conwy/Deganwy
2 Aberogwen
3 Bangor/Porth Penrhyn
4 Porth Dinorwig
5 Caernarfon
6 Foryd
15 Porthmadog/Glaslyn Dwyryd
19 Aberdyfi
25 Cardigan/Parrog
26 Porthgain
27 Solva

## Principal ports supplying and manning slate ships

7 Llanaelhaearn
8 Nefyn
9 Porth Dinllaen
10 Aberdaron
11 Rhiw
12 Abersoch
13 Pwllheli
14 Cricieth
16 Pensarn
17 Barmouth/Mawddach
18 Tywyn
20 Aberystwyth
21 Llansantffraid
22 New Quay
23 Llangrannog
24 Aberporth

## Significant River Ports

A Trefriw
B Maentwrog
C Derwen-las
D Cilgerran
E Blackpool
F St Clears

# Rail Lines of the Welsh Slate Industry

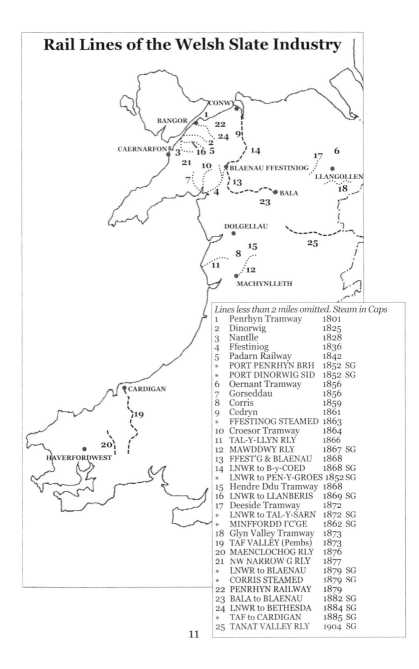

Lines less than 2 miles omitted. Steam in Caps

| | | | |
|---|---|---|---|
| 1 | Penrhyn Tramway | 1801 | |
| 2 | Dinorwig | 1825 | |
| 3 | Nantlle | 1828 | |
| 4 | Ffestiniog | 1836 | |
| 5 | Padarn Railway | 1842 | |
| * | PORT PENRHYN BRH | 1852 | SG |
| * | PORT DINORWIG SID | 1852 | SG |
| 6 | Oernant Tramway | 1856 | |
| 7 | Gorseddau | 1856 | |
| 8 | Corris | 1859 | |
| 9 | Cedryn | 1861 | |
| * | FFESTINOG STEAMED | 1863 | |
| 10 | Croesor Tramway | 1864 | |
| 11 | TAL-Y-LLYN RLY | 1866 | |
| 12 | MAWDDWY RLY | 1867 | SG |
| 13 | FFEST'G & BLAENAU | 1868 | |
| 14 | LNWR to B-y-COED | 1868 | SG |
| * | LNWR to PEN-Y-GROES | 1852 | SG |
| 15 | Hendre Ddu Tramway | 1868 | |
| 16 | LNWR to LLANBERIS | 1869 | SG |
| 17 | Deeside Tramway | 1872 | |
| * | LNWR to TAL-Y-SARN | 1872 | SG |
| * | MINFFORDD I'C'GE | 1862 | SG |
| 18 | Glyn Valley Tramway | 1873 | |
| 19 | TAF VALLEY (Pembs) | 1873 | |
| 20 | MAENCLOCHOG RLY | 1876 | |
| 21 | NW NARROW G RLY | 1877 | |
| * | LNWR to BLAENAU | 1879 | SG |
| * | CORRIS STEAMED | 1879 | SG |
| 22 | PENRHYN RAILWAY | 1879 | |
| 23 | BALA to BLAENAU | 1882 | SG |
| 24 | LNWR to BETHESDA | 1884 | SG |
| * | TAF to CARDIGAN | 1885 | SG |
| 25 | TANAT VALLEY RLY | 1904 | SG |

1

# CONWY

The Conwy, the longest and largest river wholly within Wales represented a tribal frontier in pre-Roman times. It was a source of fish not only as a foodstuff but also through its river-mussels, an occasional source of pearls that were sought in boats by the men and from the banks by the women. More notably, it was an important transport route being navigable as far upstream as its confluence with its Llugwy and Lledr tributaries at Betws-y-coed.

The Romans used slate from north-eastern Wales in the building of their fort at Caer Llugwy near Capel Curig but by medieval times Conwy was known as an important source of slate and in the 12th century may have supplied the roofing for Aberconwy Abbey. The fact that a hundred years later Edward I used slate from the Caernarfon area when building Conwy Castle, may suggest that by then the Caernarfon material was already being considered superior.

Despite a number of occurrences of slate on either side of the lower reaches of the river, those on the eastern side of the valley were generally of too doubtful quality to be tradable and on the western side ruggedness of terrain discouraged exploitation. Tal y Fan quarry SN738733 was one and possibly the only early source having a long history of sending material down to the river at Tal-y-cafn possibly by sledge.

Developed by the Normans to supply their castle, Conwy was an important port second only to Caernarfon and like Caernarfon has a record of shipbuilding from the 14th century, with great expansion during 18th century. Most builds were small sloops but many were more substantial in a variety of rigs including 2 full-rigged ships of over 200 tons. During the 19th century various shipwrights such as John Jones, John Roberts, Thomas Roberts and John Thomas had yards on the seaward side of the town wharf, building mainly schooners of less than 100 tons although John Jones' 1842 *Palanquin* was a barque of over 300 tons. By mid-century Richard Thomas emerged as the dominant builder, but by the 1860s, the railway was diminishing Conwy harbour's importance and the dearth of local timber meant that timber had to be brought in from the Baltic. Consequently after 1874 only one ship was built, the Ketch *Canovium* of 1891. Since the 1750s well over 200 vessels had been completed.

Upstream of Betws-y-coed in the Lledr, Llugwy and Machno valleys, slate was better, more abundant and more readily worked, producers there carting to Trefriw the highest practicable shipping point. From there lead, grain, wool, hide and timber were sent as far afield as Liverpool and Dublin as well as landing coal, lime and food, not forgetting wine and exotic luxuries for the gentry. Up river at Caerhun half a dozen ships were built between 1819 and 1855 and a further six between 1844 and 1874 at Trefriw itself, averaging around 50 tons and all fore-and- aft rig. But surprisingly in 1801 *Indefatigable* a brig of 154 tons had been completed at Trefriw. These obviously would have been built on informal riverside locations rather than proper yards, almost certainly by Conwy shipwrights.

By the early 19th century the increasing output of slate and of lead meant that despite the shallowness of water and the shortage of wharf space, up to 450 vessels a year were being loaded at Trefriw. In around 1812 the quay was extended which, with subsequent dredging and blasting at Tal-y-cafn enabled sea-going ships of 100 tons to be handled.

With a storehouse, a shipbuilding yard, a harbourmaster to keep everything in order and by 1854 a weighing machine and a crane, Trefriw became the most important river port in Wales, exporting by 1862 16,532 tons, ten times their 1800 figure. Although at this time lead ores provided a great deal of the tonnage this expansion was very much slate driven. Apart from the quarries in the Llugwy, Lledr and Machno valleys slate was coming in from such distant places as Rhiw-bach SH740462 and Blaen y Cwm SH745459 in such quantities that the stocking space at Trefriw was overwhelmed and ground had to be rented at Betws-y-coed to stack slate awaiting shipment. In addition, nearby slate quarries such as Clogwyn y Fuwch SH759618 and Pen y Fridd SH776612 loaded at Trefriw, a community that also provided homes and lodgings for the workers and a foundry to make repairs and spares for the various mines and quarries.

Things did not continue to go the slate men's way. By the early years of the 19th century the quality and exploitabilty of the Conwy slate was being challenged by the quarries of north-west Caernarfonshire, Blaenau Ffestiniog and elsewhere. Conwy's costs being inflated not only by the cartage charges but by the losses due to breakages carting over rough roads. In addition the Gwydir-owned Trefriw quay gave preferential rates to quarries such as Clogwyn y Fuwch and Pen y Ffridd as well as Pompren SH726519, Chwarel Ddu SH721521 and Hendre SH698512 at Dolwyddelan, who were all Gwydir tenants, disadvantaging those that were not. This encouraged the likes of Rhiw-bach and Blaen y Cwm quarries to send their product down Cwm Teigl for shipment on the Dwyryd below Maentwrog. As a consequence slate shipments were declining even ahead of the coming of the railways, would reduce the percentage of slate of Trefriw's total loadings from 70% (c1830) to 20% (c1870).

By 1836 four 'Slate to the Sea' horse/gravity railway lines were operating in northern Wales (Penrhyn, Dinorwig, Nantlle and Ffestiniog) giving the workings they served a competitive edge over cart-dependant producers. A decade later Dinorwig quarry SH595603 had put a competitive edge on a competitive edge by binning its Dinorwig line and opening its Padarn steam railway. The arrival of the Chester and Holyhead Railway at Conwy in 1848 was an additional incentive to bring forward the oft-discussed idea of a line to carry slate (as well as lead, sulphur & pyrites) from the mines and quarries of the lower Conwy valley to the port of Conwy.

The first firm proposal was the Conwy and Llanrwst Railway of 1853, which envisaged a 3' gauge, locomotive line from an interchange at Conwy station, to run along the western side of the valley to Trefriw, crossing the river just north of Llanrwst to service that town. Branches would be laid to mines in the Gwydir forest and the slate workings in Cwm Eigiau. A horse-drawn extension would reach Betws-y-coed where it would branch three ways to serve Hafodlas quarry SH779562, the various quarries at Dolwyddelan and Cwm Machno. Probably because it was realised that no way could Conwy's limited port facilities handle the sort of tonnages that were envisaged, there seems to have been no provision to take slate to the quayside. Although by this time there were standard gauge branches to both Porth Penrhyn and Porth Dinorwig to pick up slate brought down from their respective quarries, rail freight was generally considered too costly for the conveyance of slate, so the lack of shipping capabilities may have been why this proposal failed to find backers. This plan was followed in 1858 by another for a line to Llanrwst following the same, mainly west bank route without branches or extensions, but beefed up to 3' 3" gauge. Despite being promoted by the redoubtable Hugh Beaver Roberts, the great tramway pioneer, it too failed to win support. It is interesting that both these shunned standard gauge, cost considerations (Double the gauge, quadruple the cost), taking precedence over the avoidance of the extra handling at the main line interchange.

In 1860 the London and North Western Railway, an amalgamation that created the then largest joint-stock company in the world, absorbed the Chester and Holyhead and put a stop to these local ideas by planning their own standard gauge branch up the eastern side of the valley from what was to become Llandudno Junction. The east river bank was chosen because of the difficulty of laying out a junction to the west of Stephenson's rail bridge and to avoid bridging to reach Llanrwst, which was the great commercial prize. Also the impossibility of expanding the Conwy quay meant that if additional shipment capacity was required it would have to be created on the east bank of the river.

The line opened to Llanrwst in 1863, great for that important market town but of little value to the slate producers on the lower Conwy since it was on the wrong side of the valley for their quarries. One can understand the railway company's thinking – few of these quarries were seen as likely to produce more than a couple of truck loads per week.

Although this new Conwy & Llanrwst Railway had neither plans nor authorisation to go beyond Llanrwst, William Dew a partner in Hafodlas quarry SN779562 wrote in 1862, -"There is no question that it (the railway) will shortly be extended to pass the foot of our incline". That same year, and presumably with the same expectations, Foel quarry SH717556 constructed the fine Moel Siabod Tramway. Of 2' gauge and 1½ miles long, it left the quarry by an incline from the foot of which it ran by gravity (with horse return) to the head of an incline system of one long shallow pitch and two shorter, steep pitches, reaching the road at Pont Cyfyng about 800' below. Shortly after opening, the lowest pitch was extended to a riverside mill. (From 1874 the system also carried output from Rhos quarry SH729564 by way of a feeder which joined part way down the long incline).

Of course there never was the William Dew predicted railway along the Llugwy valley and a more realistic view of transport was taken by Cedryn quarry SH719635 high in the fastnesses of Carnedd Llywelyn' when it was redeveloped in 1861 – they built their own tramway to a new wharf on the river at Dolgarrog.

The Cedryn Tramway was of 2' gauge and 4 miles long, horse/gravity worked, beginning at the foot of an incline from the quarry. It followed a gentle down grade for 1¾ miles, where at the end of a stone embankment it dropped to ground level by the short Pwll Ddu incline. From there it continued for 1¼ miles to the lip of the hanging valley. The valley floor some 850' below was reached by a three pitch incline, the two upper pitches end on, the lowest turning slightly northward to dive under the road. From there a ½ mile run across the Conwy flood plain took it to a wharf on the grandly named Porth Llwyd. (This final part of the line was relaid during the 1906/7 constructions of the Aluminium works as a temporary tramway).

By 1864 the Cedryn line had been extended ¾ mile to Cwm Eigiau quarry SH702635. This extension also served a new Cedryn mill that due to water constraints had to be remotely sited and connected to the quarry by a viaduct.

The railway remained resolutely terminated at Llanrwst, much to the benefit of the town, but with little prospect of worthwhile freight revenues. It was only after almost five years that the line was extended to Betws-y-coed and appropriately renamed as the Llandudno Junction to Betws-y-coed branch, opening for goods in 1867 and passengers in 1868. That same year St. George's pier and harbour at Deganwy was opened, to act as a new east bank port for Conwy readily served by a spur from the L&NWR Llandudno Junction – Llandudno branch.

The Betws-y-coed terminus of the L&NWR enabled quarries such as Cwm Machno, SH751470, Foel/Rhos, Hafodlas and the Lledr valley workings around Dolwyddelan to shorten their cartages, avoid the congestion at Trefriw and as railway users could ship toll-free at Deganwy. Slate apart, the Betws connection made that town a focus for the Lledr, Llugwy, Machno and upper Conwy valleys and a centre for the lead mining of the Gwydir Forest. Passenger services apart from ending the isolation of Betws also opened it up as an important tourist town. The L&NWR realised that there was not enough potential traffic to justify building lines up the Llugwy and Machno valleys, particularly as seemed every likelihood that others would do so, thus giving the railway company additional traffic without additional expenditure.

This was to an extent a high-risk strategy. Had Hafodlas' rumblings about running rails the half-mile or so to Betws-y-coed station come to anything, all well and good but in the event Hafodlas never had the money to pay for it nor the traffic to justify it. Alternative schemes could have been a different matter. For instance had the General Undertaking of the North Wales Narrow Gauge Railway plans for a line up the Glaslyn valley and on to Betws-y-coed been built it could have picked up Hafodlas and Foel/Rhos traffic, but had its Beddgelert-Porthmadog section also been completed, slate could just as easily been taken to Porthmadog, either for shipping or to transfer to the Cambrian Railways. The Machno branch of the proposed Corwen-Betws-y-coed section of the grand NWNGR plan could have picked up shedloads of slate from the Cwm Machno quarries, but could well have taken it not to the L&NWR at Betws-y-coed, but to the Great Western Railway at Corwen.

In the meantime other areas were gaining advantage by the opening of three further horse/gravity slate railways, the

Gorseddau, the Croesor to Porthmadog, and the Corris, Machynlleth and River Dyfi to Derwen-las. More seriously, the Tal-y-llyn steam railway had opened and the Ffestiniog had not only been steamed but was boosted by new feeder lines. All of which more than doubled to almost forty the number of sizeable slate quarries that had direct rail connection.

The Conwy valley railway was successful in picking up slate at Betws-y-coed, but the real prize was Blaenau Ffestiniog where more slate than even the largest of the Conwy quarries produced in a year was being dispatched on a daily basis. Moreover this slate was being carried by a 'toy' railway whose charges reflected its monopoly status and being taken to a port (Porthmadog) that was fast becoming woefully inadequate and lacked direct connection to a 'proper' railway. The thought of hundreds of tons of slate awaiting transport at quarries less than a dozen miles from their railhead must have caused collective apoplexy in the Euston boardroom of the L&NWR!

Unfortunately although the branch had reached Betws with a minimum of civil engineering, a very large lump of rock, the diamond-hard Moel Dyrnogydd, stood in the way of progress to Blaenau. There were two possible routes, up the Lledr valley and tunnel for 2 miles or up the Machno valley a longer route but with a marginally shorter tunnel – what may have been the decider for the former route may have been the greater slate potential of the Lledr valley as compared with the Machno. The extension was originally planned to be of 2' gauge, giving a considerable saving in the tunnelling costs. It would not have been much of a disadvantage for slate traffic since the Deganwy dock had been designed to accept narrow gauge quarry wagons so that these would then have been loaded onto transporter trucks at Betws rather than Blaenau. Similarly slate intended for rail distribution would have been transferred to main line wagons at Betws rather than Blaenau and direct connection to the Ffestiniog Railway would have made it easier to siphon off its traffic. However avoiding a break of gauge at Betws would greatly increase the potential for delivering goods and passenger traffic into the burgeoning Blaenau.

Commenced in 1872 in standard gauge, the Blaenau Ffestiniog extension took seven years to build, a delay that removed all hope of great profitability. Apart from the fact that the Ffestiniog Railway's 1863 steaming had much increased its efficiency, the Cambrian Railways had established the huge Minffordd interchange within months of the commencement of work on the L&NWR extension, thus greatly facilitating the loading of Blaenau slate onto the Cambrian and providing stocking space that eased the crush at Porthmadog harbour. More importantly, by 1879 when the new line opened to Blaenau the slate trade was tailspinning into recession.

Llechwedd quarry SH700470 seeing an opportunity to put one over the Ffestiniog Railway immediately took a spur off of their incline down to the Ffestiniog Railway, to reach a new commodious stockyard served by a siding off the new L&NWR line. Shortly afterwards Oakeley SH691470 built a similar but smaller arrangement (Later augmented by a line to the L&NWR station) and at Blaenau itself other quarries could access the new L&NWR terminus via a link to the FR. Although cornucopian tonnages never ensued, some benefit was reaped in the 1890s when Blaenau boomed. The Deganwy harbour had received a possibly unforeseen bonus when the L&NWR opened their Llanberis branch in 1869 bringing a great deal of slate traffic from Llanberis that by-passed the Caernarfon quays to take advantage of Deganwy's L&NWR ownership to load free of port-duties.

Although slate tonnages on the L&NWR (Later LMS) line may not have reached hoped-for proportions, by the end of the 19th century a substantial amount of stone from the Blaenau granite workings was being carried. In addition its social impact was great, putting Blaenau in touch with Caernarfonshire for the first time and linking what had become by far the largest town in north-western Wales into the national railway network.

The completion of the Conwy valley railway did not put an end to ideas for laying rails on the western side of the river, not only to pick up slate, and lead as well as pyrites from the Caecoch sulphur mine SH775654 but also for passenger traffic. The railway having robbed Trefriw of much of its freight traffic, it set about reinventing itself as a holiday destination, with the expectation at the height of the late 19th century fashion for 'Taking the Waters', to use the Chalybeate springs to challenge the likes of Harrogate and Llandrindod. Accordingly, in 1868 Hugh Beaver Roberts, flush from his success with the Croesor tramway sought support for a standard gauge revival of his west bank scheme of a decade before. This having failed, there was a proposal in the late 1870s for a narrow gauge rail connection from Llanrwst station to Trefriw. Some formations were laid out, (traceable as paths with the Gower footbridge at SH792622 marking the site of the river crossing). Although revenues were predicted to predominately come from posh passengers the figures did not add up without an appreciable freight element, hence the slate trade recession put a stopper on the plan. The idea of rails to Trefriw for passengers at least, was raised again in 1907 when a standard gauge branch crossed the river to serve the Aluminium works at Dolgarrog. It was suggested that an electric tramway could use the bridge to link a new station on the L&NWR with Trefriw. This idea was abandoned in favour of the Conwy Valley Light Railway proposal which was a standard gauge edition of Roberts' 1868 west bank line. This plan was only abandoned post WW1, when serious slate working, most other industry and widespread belief in the curative power of spa waters was history. In 2010 a revival of the bridge link line was proposed.

Oddly despite being deprived of the rail connection considered vital to slate working, both Rhos and Cwm Machno not only prospered unconnected, but proved surprisingly durable surviving into the 1960s, only closing due to a shortage of skilled labour.

As regards communities there were several but all were small. Cwm Machno, Dolweddelan and to a lesser extent Capel Currig were slate villages but at Betws-y-coed the slate influence was limited. However the neighbouring tiny community of Rhiwddolion was totally a quarry village and remained so even after the quarry closed since the workforce en-bloc transferred to Blaenau Ffestiniog, catching the train at Pont y Pant. Trefriw's slate connection was too diluted by its mining and spa activities to be classed as a slate settlement and slate had little impact on Conwy town itself and although Deganwy shipped slate in some quantity, the port never generated a slate related infrastructure. In fact slate activity in the whole region was too small and too dispersed to develop the foundries, engineering expertise and suppliers etc, which supported other regions. Similarly maritime activity was never enough to generate industries such as block and rope makers, chandlers and such on a scale that aided shipbuilding and operation at other ports.

The most important community that was at least partially and indirectly slate created was Llandudno Junction that developed engineering expertise arising out of the substantial locomotive workshops, but it was the 1920s before it found a slate role, with the establishment of the Colloidal Slate Co.

Slate regarded as smart in Victorian times had by the 1920s come to being associated with drab workers' terraces. Sales of Westmorland and Pembrokeshire's green slates had thanks to aggressive marketing, held up well despite their cost. Thus there was the feeling that if north Wales slates could be sold in green all would be well. In a rare burst of co-operation Penrhyn Quarry and Dinorwig quarry, in northwest Caernarfonshire joined with Oakeley quarry at Blaenau to set up the Colloidal Slate Company, Llandudno Junction being chosen as it was on a major railway and midway between Blaenau and the Caernarfonshire quarries. This firm could coat slate in green, brown, buff, terra cotta and red. It was at pains to point out that it was not merely 'paint' but was by a 'secret Colloidal process' and was 'absolutely permanent'. There seems to have been two drawbacks – it proved impermanent and although it could be profitably sold only some 14 % above the cost of uncoated slate and a useful near third below Westmorland slate, it still was dearer than tiles in most markets. Penrhyn and Dinorwig dropped out in the mid-1930s leaving Oakeley in sole charge, they closed the factory during WW2, finally winding up in 1948.

Llandudno Junction was a double junction (One branch to Llandudno, one to Blaenau Ffestiniog) and can boast that half a century after Dr. Beeching wielded his axe it is still a double junction. It no longer has its famous loco sheds but still hosts light industry, although the biggest employer is now an outstation of the Welsh Assembly.

2

# BANGOR and PORTH PENRHYN

This area is famous for having the first railway ever to be laid down solely for the carriage of slate although in fact it nearly never had a railway at all since in the mindset of the late 18th century the canal was the only way to move goods in bulk. Therefore Lord Penrhyn whose eponymous quarry at Bethesda virtually monopolised the area, being fed up with troublesome carters, commanded that plans for a canal be drawn up to convey slate from his quarry to his new harbour at Porth Penrhyn. Never a man to accept second best, he picked Thomas Dadford the premier canal engineer of the day to prepare a survey. With a fall of 600' in six miles it is unlikely that Dadford thought much of the idea himself, but if Lord Penrhyn said he wanted a canal, a canal it would have to be. Locks were not an option since it would have needed anything up to sixty of them so Dadford came up with the idea of nine reaches linked by eight inclined planes down which loaded barges could be lowered by ropes and up which teams of horses could haul the empties. Eventually of course his Lordship saw that such a canal was non-starter and in 1801 his quarry was connected to Porth Penrhyn by the famously pioneering railway.

However prior to this, a lot had gone on in the Ogwen valley. Some of the earliest successful slate working in Britain if not the world was carried out at Cae Braich y Cefn on the barren northern slopes of Mynydd Elidir at SH620650, somewhere near the present quarry's offices. Slate was probably dug here in Roman times and later may have been monastically worked, but by the 18th century it was won by small informal partnerships, *gweithio ar y cyd* (joint working) who carried their output to a shipping point at Aberogwen in animal pannier-baskets. These diggings were on land 'incorporated' into the Penrhyn Estate that not unreasonably expected to collect tribute from the diggers. Since such royalties were based on the tonnage of slate produced, the Estate had a vested interest in the diggers keeping busy. Unfortunately by the mid-18th century there was increasing competition from the slatemen of Cilgwyn and Cefn Ddu (between the Nantlle and the Gwyrfai and Padarn valleys respectively). Generally their rock was better and produced thinner slates that commanded a higher price than the Ogwen material, being lighter they cost less to transport and anyway their journey to the coast was shorter. The clincher was that these men operated on Crown land where royalties seemed to have been but rarely collected.

Little wonder than that the diggers were abandoning their Penrhyn workings and joining the Cilgwyn and Cefn Ddu men where they could easily double their weekly takings. To discourage this drift the Penrhyn estate reduced royalties, and facilitated trade by standardising sizes, a brilliant move that was immediately copied by their competitors. But despite the Estate's best efforts, by the mid 18th century the Cilgwyn/Cefn Du men were turning out several times the total being raised on Penrhyn land.

In 1765 Susanna daughter of General Warburton majority owner of the Penrhyn Estate married Richard Pennant son of a wealthy Liverpool merchant. He and his father-in-law set about sorting things out. They cancelled every digger's take note, issued long leases at a flat-rate rent that gave the tenants confidence to develop their workings. This they most certainly did and by the time the General died in 1781 Richard found himself the ground landlord of a thriving industry. Unfortunately the aggregate of the dead-rents of £70 per annum that had seemed reasonable a decade or so earlier, was now derisory compared with the money that the tenants were making thanks to increased selling prices and a spiralling demand from their main Liverpool market. The notion of tenants prospering was totally anathematic to Richard Pennant (or Lord Penrhyn of the First Creation as one would shortly need to call him), so he bought out the 54 leases in 1782 and started to work the sett himself. Using his father's Liverpool connections he engaged Samuel Worthington, an influential Liverpool businessman to buy the diggers' output and aggressively market the product. Shipment was concentrated at Cegin Pool wharf, Abercegin that had been increasingly used as an alternative to Aberogwen since 1713. The Cegin pool wharf was later abandoned and a port was developed on the seaward side of it on a scale that would have been impossible at Aberogwen and the lot grandly named Porth Penrhyn. A direct, well-surfaced road was built to it in 1790 obviating the use of pack animals, (Now approximately the B4409) whilst this did not dramatically reduce cartage costs (20p per ton instead of 27p) it reduced breakages and greatly speeded up the journeys especially in winter. Soon their tonnage was double that of Cilgwyn.

Porth Penrhyn was not only the first dedicated slate port but also became the first slate orientated 'Industrial estate'. Paradoxically although it would shortly have a vast writing slate factory, other slate processing mills turning out tombstones and slab, as well as a foundry, its initial industrial development was not slate connected but would provide a prototype for slate transport.

This first Port Penrhyn industry was a flint calcining plant set up by Worthington in the 1790s in connection with his

Liverpool pottery, the attraction being that coal and flint could be cheaply brought in by slate vessels as a return cargo and the established shipping route to Liverpool could be used to deliver the calcined material. This might have been a nice little earner had there been water available to him on site to power a grinding mill. As it was the mill had to be built in the Ogwen valley, connected to the port by a railway. The railway was by no means a pioneer, wagon ways were a well established tool in heavy industry and mining, but perhaps not on as tricky a route as this. Trucks carrying the flint had to be hauled up an incline, pulled for three- quarters of a mile, then lowered down another incline to the mill. Then the ground-up slurries had to be returned to Porth Penrhyn for calcining by the same route. The inclines were powered by horse-whims and since they were over-engineered and under-used the whole scheme was uneconomic, even when the use was augmented by flax seed that Worthington was grinding in the Ogwen mill for his paint factory at Porth Penrhyn. When it came to improving the slate carriage arrangements, one can forgive Lord Penrhyn's shunning of a seemingly clanking monstrosity like Worthington's tramway in favour of a canal, anyway in the last decade or so of the 18th century everyone was building canals, tramways being considered suitable only for short and relatively light feeder roles and definitely unsuited to the sort of tonnages that he expected to be shifting.

When it was wisely decided that a canal was a no-no Dadford produced plans for a tramway. A gauge of 4' or so was established practice in the coal and iron industries, a dimension that owed more to the size and capabilities of a horse rather than the anecdotal spacing of Roman chariot wheels, but wagons of this gauge could not be conveniently manhandled within the confines of a quarry. Dadford suggested a gauge of 5' 2", presumably with the intention of carrying narrow-gauge quarry wagons pic-a-back. He conformed to the fashion of the time in specifying 'L' section tram plates and narrow wagon wheels, rather than the then less popular edge rails and flanged wheels, but to maintain acceptable gradients inclines would still be required. In contrast with the flint mill inclines that handled roughly the same loads in each direction, the quarry line inclines would be only lowering loaded wagons, raising being confined to empties and to comparatively trivial tonnages of supplies, so could be self acting with the weight of down-going loaded wagons up-hauling empty ones on a parallel track. The self-acting incline had been patented by a Michael Meinzies in 1750 but strength and stretch of hemp ropes restricted pitch lengths until wire ropes became available in the mid-19th century. Therefore chains, which were just coming into widespread use following their recent adoption by the Navy, were specified. Vertical line-side sheaves at the head of the inclines were proposed, presumably based on the horse-whim powered arrangements on the flint mill line. With the French wars having stagnated trade in the 1790s the industry was in no mood to invest, but despite his recent output of 11,000 tons per annum having taken a serious hit, much by the loss of Irish trade, Lord Penrhyn, confident that the good times would return, set about building the line using the quarrymen whom the slump had made idle. He was of course right, the 1801 opening of the Penrhyn Railroad was just in time for the return of confidence that followed the Treaty of Amiens in 1802.

Penrhyn agent Benjamin Wyatt, was charged with the actual construction and he adopted a gauge of 24½" (over rail centres) which was probably already in use on the flint mill line. Such a gauge minimised construction costs, used trucks that could be manhandled within the quarry and gave a handy size of wagon for working the inclines. It is probable that

Wyatt recognised the inherent soundness of the flint mill line and hence followed its practice. Less well advised was his choice of track. He did not like tram plates since he believed such track could not be properly 'gravelled'. Nor did he like stone blocks since they could not accurately maintain gauge. Accordingly he specified edge rails raised well up on 'sills' (integral chair/sleepers) that were kinked to lay well below ballast level where they could not trip up the horses. So far so good but he specified a double-flanged wheel layout which Dadford had tried in south Wales but had abandoned in favour of the Outram L-plate. Wyatt's version had oval section rail on which ran wheels with a concave rim of slightly greater radius than the upper surface of the rail thus offering almost point contact, - until wear having made the radii identical causing the wheels to jam on the rails. Curiously he used wheels fixed to the axle, unnecessary with what was effectively a double-flanged layout, this was also a source of jamming due to distortion and/or manufacturing tolerance failing to keep the rails exactly to gauge, plus the differing distance covered by the inner and outer wheels on a curve caused drag and accelerated wear. In addition at 14" diameter the wheels were smaller than would have been ideal.

The line ran from Coed y Parc, just below the quarry for about a mile to the Cilgeraint incline at SH613669 that dropped it 63'. A further 1½ miles took it to the Dinas incline at SH610684 dropping it 58'. After another almost 3 miles, having joined the route of the flint mill tramway at Llandegai near the head of its incline at SH589708 to Aberogwen, dropped a further 102' on the Marchogion incline at SH595719 (which it substantially took over from the flint line) and thence about ¾ mile to the port. The river Cegin was crossed and recrossed, firstly using a pre-existing single-arched road bridge and secondly by a wooden bridge (replaced in 1820 by a fine three arched bridge).

On all the inclines wagons were crewled three at a time. The non-incline sections had an almost constant fall of a little over 1 in 100, assisting the loaded journeys without greatly impeding the return of empties, which together with the well separated inclines, gave it an ideal layout. It was claimed that even with the delays of crewling wagons on the inclines, six trains of up to 24 wagons, each carrying up to a ton, drawn by 2 or 3 horses, could pass each way daily giving a theoretical capacity of some 40,000 tons per annum, way over the foreseeable output of the quarry. A near contemporary account stated that only 16 horses were required to replace the 400 needed to draw the carts. This is possibly an exaggeration, but nevertheless a dramatic reduction in both horse and man power was achieved.

The line gave Penrhyn quarry a uniquely cheap and reliable route to the sea. Apart from dramatically facilitating the dispatch of finished slate, it eased the bringing in of timber, building materials and so on. In due course as mechanisation of the quarry developed, its ability to carry machinery, engineering supplies and coal would become vital.

A year after the tramway opened a writing slate factory was established at Porth Penrhyn, with a timber sawmill to produce the frames being erected below the flint mill at Aberogwen, all of which set Porth Penrhyn on the way to being an industrial site in its own right, with independent slate merchant/processors such as Dixon & Co and Thomas & Co, setting up there. Such was the increase in slate production that only three years after rail connection, the harbour was enlarged (using slate waste brought down from the quarry by rail). By 1820 the Cegin Pool was abandoned enabling the two sides of the port to be joined by a fine iron road bridge.

The line's considerable overcapacity proved fortunate as the idiosyncratic rails caused delays. Substantial track replacement had been carried out by 1821 when part of the route at Llandegai was re-aligned enabling the new turnpike to be underpassed eliminating a level crossing. The old rails and their iron sleepers were replaced by conventional edge rails and wooden sleepers on 1'10¾" gauge. Later the vertical drums and chains of the inclines were replaced by the more usual horizontal drums and wire ropes.

In spite of the problems, it has been estimated that the line enabled a ton of slate to reach the port at a cost of 5p against 20p (or more) by cart. An appreciable saving on products that could sell for less than £1 per ton.

This pioneering rail/port arrangement that lasted unchanged for half a century, enabled the Penrhyn quarry to establish dominance over the Welsh slate trade that persists to this day. In 1852 the scope of the port was widened when a branch from the London and North Western Railway (Neé Chester to Holyhead Railway) was laid to Porth Penrhyn. Since Penrhyn's trade was so closely linked to Liverpool, significant tonnages soon were going there by rail rather than sea, both for the north of England trade and for loading on ships too big for Porth Penrhyn's limited capacity. Paradoxically this rail connection far from harming Porth Penrhyn enhanced it, since the railway facilitated the coaling and servicing of steam ships, enabling a fleet of quarry-owned steamers to be based here. This embracing of the steamer may well have helped to maintain the port's credibility when the rug was pulled from under it by the 1900-1903 stoppage, and ultimately keep the port functioning into the 21st century, still shipping occasional loads of powdered slate.

Porth Penrhyn cannot be considered other than in conjunction with Bangor itself. Probably long before Abercegin was handling Penrhyn output, the product of other quarries was being carried by oxen driven by young girls to load at Hireal. Before a quay was built in 1821 this would have been done at low tide into vessels drawn up onto the beach.

Bangor had been little more than a cathedral-dependent village, but slate and Telford's Irish Road doubled its population between 1801 and 1821 and redoubled it between 1821 and 1841 finally peaking in 1861 at 10,000. The later growth was partly railway driven, especial as it eventually covered five junctions (Caernarfon, Bethesda, Porth Penrhyn, Porth Dinorwig and Amlwch) and the Britannia Bridge. Having in addition engine sheds and a big goods depot with a fleet of horse-drays meant that eventually the L&NWR Bangor payroll almost topped 500.

To cater for larger vessels especially steamers, a jetty was built at Garth in 1891, just to the east of where the pier would be built a few years later. Despite the presence of the railway this jetty continued to be used until the 1930s by coastal ships such as those of Messrs David Jones & Co making their regular deliveries from Liverpool to the grocers of Bangor.

Although some small vessels were built at Bangor in the 16th & 17th centuries, building remained sporadic up to the 1820s despite the 18th century expansion of the slate trade. This was partly due to the availability of both ships and crews from places down the coast such as Nefyn, (whose eventual build total was double that of Bangor). However the lack of need for builds was chiefly due to the availability of ships from Amlwch since the decline of the Parys copper trade almost exactly matched the rise of slate. The further rise of the slate trade encouraged the setting up of the big Hirael yards, John Robert's, beside the mouth of the River Adda, John Parry's (formerly John Jones, later T. T. Parry) opposite the Nelson Arms and Edward Ellis's, where Dickie's yard still operates. In addition to these 'proper' yards with sawing and forging and other facilities; there were several 'One off' builds on Hirael beach. Between 1775 and 1879 when the last ship the

32

38-ton smack *Pilgrim* was built by T. T. Parry, just over 60 vessels were completed almost all being fore-and-aft rig. Few exceeded 100 tons, the largest at 258 tons more than twice the size of any other was Edward Ellis' 1859 Barque *Heather Bell*. Overwhelmingly the slate carried was from Penrhyn whose trade was mainly with Liverpool and the Irish Sea, so voyages were short thus for a given annual tonnage the shipping space needs were smaller than world-range ports such as Porthmadog.

Up to the end of the 18th century ships tended to be owned by wealthy landowners, but from the early 1800s, business and professional men speculated in shipping. The senior management of Penrhyn quarry such as Worthington, Wyatt, Williams the Reeve who oversaw the Port and Greenfield the quarry engineer, took shares in vessels. Commercial firms such as Worthington's Liverpool partnership with Samuel Holland and Michael Humble began to own ships and in fact this syndicate rented part of a quay at Porth Penrhyn. It is interesting that Samuel Holland later branched out independently seeking slate supplies by buying a small quarry at Blaenau Ffestiniog that he famously sent his son to manage in 1818.

Gradually professional men, farmers, shopkeepers and even quarrymen took a few sixty-fourths of a ship or two and it was commonplace for a big shipbuilder to retain a share in a vessel as part payment.

It seems that John Mann the butler at Penrhyn Castle invested in ships – having one's soup served by a ship owner must have surely been the ultimate dinner party conversation piece! The Penrhyns themselves were of course ship owners, their Anglesey Shipping Company having a fleet of steam ships, the last the *Sybil Mary* being sold off in the mid 1950s. There were several other shipping 'lines' based at Bangor but these rarely owned more than just the one ship.

Besides the ancillary industries at Porth Penrhyn, there were a number at Bangor town. There were several manufacturing slate merchants such as William Jones, Holyhead Road, Thomas & Co High Street, John Thomas & Son, Mountain Square, who specialised in ridges and had an enamelling kiln, Humphrey Williams at Hirael and Williams at Garth who also turned out ridges and enamelled work - plus of course the great E J J Dixon whose produce at their Station Square works included school writing slates and ridges. The present contracting firm of John Williams & Co, although having English connections, can trace its roots back to a 1870s Bangor manufacturing merchant.

It has always been said of the slate industry that when times are bad no one has the money to modernise, and when times are good no time to do so. Certainly as far as transport was concerned Penrhyn quarry was struggling on with an outdated tramway that by the 1860s was groaning under throughputs more than double those envisaged by its builders. Before the end of the decade the Ffestiniog Railway, the Tal-y-llyn Railway and the Ffestiniog and Blaenau Railway had joined Dinorwig in showing that steam was the only way to power such a line. In addition the Nantlle Railway that served their old rivals on Cefn Du had in effect been partly steamed. It was obvious that to move over 1000 tons per week by horses and gravity inclines was 'No way to run a railroad'. There were ideas of totally abandoning the existing tramway and relying on the standard gauge layout linking the quarry, the port, Bangor town and Bethesda that the L&NWR were rumoured to be planning, at the same time there were speculations that the branch to Ffestiniog that the Great Western were known to be planning might push on to serve Penrhyn and Dinorwig. In the end it was recognised that the existing railway would have to be steamed.

In fairness replacing an old railway with a new one on substantially the same route without interfering with the flow of traffic was a challenge, particularly since by the time work was started in early 1876, come what may the better part of 350 tons had to be brought down to the port each and every working day. The incline-less Ffestiniog had to do little more than to replace the track, the Tal-y-llyn had been a new build, and the Padarn Railway had taken a totally different route from the Dinorwig horse line that it replaced. The Penrhyn rebuild had to make deviations to avoid the three inclines, but fortunately the main confliction was confined to the stretch from the quarry at Coed y Parc to the top of the Cilgeraint incline, even so it was almost 3½ years before the new line was fully open.

From the head of the Cilgeraint incline a new line swung in a great loop to bypass both that incline and the Dinas incline to drop into the Cegin valley totally clear of the Marchoglion incline. Crossing the river early, it bridged the old route with a new span and crossed the Cegin by widening the bridge that carried the standard gauge port branch. Actually there was a slight miscalculation on this bridge sharing, a standard gauge locomotive could pass a narrow gauge train, but with their widely projecting cylinders a narrow-gauge loco was never able to pass a standard gauge train. Workmen's trains on this new line now less transat-lantically defined as a Railway rather than Railroad, started in 1880 and having five intermediate stops offered increased opportunities for 'off site' living.

By this time workers employed at Penrhyn quarry and their families numbered many thousands. Senior employees tended to live in the Penrhyn owned showpiece garden-village of Llandegai, others in the several quarry-owned terraces, once reviled as little more than prison cells but now are prized as bijou second homes. Others lived in self-build cottage smallholdings on Penrhyn land often using materials given them by the quarry. Those preferring to have their dwellings outside quarry control set up possibly in places such as Rachub or Tregarth, usually with a plot of land attached.

However the majority lived in Bethesda, which had grown up on non-Penrhyn land along Telford's Irish Road (A5) to become a considerable town. Despite the fact that by the 1890s almost every town of consequence in Britain was rail connected, Bethesda was not (the new steam line was only open to employees). This was mainly due to the influence of the successive owners of Penrhyn quarry and in particular the current one, the 1st Baron Penrhyn (of the second creation). Apart from wishing to deprive competitors of rail freight opportunities, a lack of rail travel restricted their employees' opportunities to find work elsewhere and thus maintain the Penrhyn quarry's monopoly employer situation. Towards the end of the 1870s when the pressure for a public rail service became overwhelming, the Baron offered to extend the quarry railway across the valley to Bethesda and provide freight and passenger services. This really was unacceptable, for not only would it give the Penrhyns control over and veto on who and what was carried but also any passenger interchange at Porth Penrhyn would have been problematical.

Eventually in 1884 the L&NWR devised a route to Bethesda from a junction at Llandegai that avoided Penrhyn land. The tunnelling and bridging proved costly and almost as nearly as tedious as the negotiations. Space for a terminus was only found by flattening the tip of the independent Coetmor quarry whose closure a few years earlier had been partially precipitated by the lack of a railway.

Paradoxically this line that the Lords Penrhyn had so resolutely opposed because of its facilitation of the movement of labour, proved invaluable to Lord Penrhyn when during the

1900-1903 stoppage he needed to bring in outside labour.

Actually the Bethesda branch despite serving what is arguably the most famous slate town in the world, can scarcely be classed as a slate railway. The largest independent quarry Bryn Hafod y Wern SN631693 was hard hit by the 1870s slump and closed totally when the Penrhyns cut off their water supply. This left Pantdreiniog SN623671, Moelfaban SN626679 and Tanybwlch SN628683 as the only quarries working on more than a 'Two men and a dog' scale and their combined outputs were unexciting.

With one near monopoly producer controlling transport, downstream activities such as slab sawing, tile making and slate powder grinding as well as supply and services were kept 'in house'. Thus independent slate works did not develop in Bethesda, there being only one small slate mill owned by Richard Owen possibly with just a single saw. There was one chandler dealing with sundry supplies, but when his face ceased to fit at Penrhyn quarry, he went bust. Again as a result of isolation until the belated arrival of the railway, other commercial activities did not develop and certainly Bethesda did not see visitors in the numbers that Llanberis was able (and still is able) to attract.

With buses able to offer much faster travel and even putting men from say Anglesey who hitherto had been weekly barrackers, less than an hour from home. Workmen's trains on the Penrhyn Railway ceased in 1951 but the line continued to carry slate until 1962, so if one regards the steam line as a continuation of the horse/gravity line, it was not only the first but also the last 'slate railway' to actually carry slate. The standard gauge line to Porth Penrhyn closed in 1963 but the port has avoided 'Marinaisation' and continues in occasional commercial use.

# 3

# PORTH DINORWIG

The Faenol estate was not as extensive as the Penrhyn estate, but it still occupied a goodly slice of northwestern Caernarfonshire including a swathe of the southern flank of Mynydd Elidir where, like Penrhyn on the northern side, an otherwise pretty useless tract was let to slate diggers. Faenol's late 18th century custodian Thomas Assheton-Smith (Snr) was a less prominent man than his Penrhyn counterpart, but could claim that much of his wealth was less controversially acquired. Deriving not from sugar plantations but from the quick thinking of an ancestor. The tale is that bizarrely a William Williams left land to King William III, who allegedly scoffed at a bequest of what he was told was "barren rock". As soon as it became known that the King did not want it, Assheton-Smith's ancestor John Smith then the Speaker of the Commons allegedly cried "Bags me!"

Whatever the source of his land Assheton-Smith was just as anxious to maximise its yield. Seeing the success that Lord Penrhyn was enjoying from having taken the diggings into his own hand he bought out his own diggers' leases in 1787. However being less affluent he could not make the outlays nor take the risks that Penrhyn could, so he reduced his exposure by forming the Dinorwig Slate Company, in partnership with his agent Thomas Wright, his solicitor Hugh Ellis another lawyer and William Bridges a slate merchant who had been handling sales of the tenants' output.

They were not as successful as the Penrhyn organisation, nor could they hope to be with their unsatisfactory transport arrangements. Slate was sent down inclines to be loaded onto boats on Llyn Padarn, which were then rowed to the end of the lake at Cwm-y-glo to be carted to Caernarfon. Admittedly this was better than the traditional route whereby output was sent by pack animal and loaded onto carts at Penisa'waen SH558640 where a road of sorts could be found, but even so this new route was still cumbersome. Despite their best efforts, at the outbreak of the French wars in 1793 their tonnage was less than a quarter that of Penrhyn. There was some improvement from the mid 1790s when shipment was increasingly made at Aberpwll, the creek used by the Anglesey ferry, which not only shortened the carriage but also being on Faenol land escaped port dues. Improvements here in 1802 enabled the use of Caernarfon to be abandoned.

The Dinorwig Company held up better than Penrhyn during the difficult wartime conditions of the late 1790s and expanded in the first years of the new century and began to look like real challengers to Penrhyn, much of whose big Irish trade had been lost. In 1807 encouraged by this and anticipating the expiry of the Company's lease the following year, Assheton-Smith set about drastically improving communication between the quarry and the sea. Possibly deterred from considering a railway by the troubles Penrhyn were having with their track, he pressed ahead with a grand cart road through Dinorwig village and the then nascent settlement of Ebenezer (now Deiniolen) (Substantially the route of A4244/B4547), to his new Porth Dinorwig at Y Felinheli as Aberpwll was beginning to be called. From there regular shipments were made mainly in local vessels predominantly to ports such as Liverpool, Chester or Preston all of which gave access to the English canal system. In addition some sales were being made further afield and ships from even the then infant United States were calling at Porth Dinorwig to load slates.

When in 1808 the lease did expire, presumably feeling he could afford to up his stake, Assheton-Smith reformed the Dinorwig Company with the help of banker Hugh Jones and William Turner, headhunted from Blaenau to provide the expertise, but with himself firmly in control. Further improvements were made to both the port and the roads that by 1812 could be considered complete and well surfaced. To help the latter stay that way, carriers were offered incentives to use broad wheels on their carts to minimise wear. Even so transport costs and general efficiency both lagged behind Penrhyn and with trade turning sour from 1815, this needed attention, but Assheton-Smith continued to shun rails. However his son Thomas (jnr) was having an increasing say in the quarry affairs and presumably through his influence a railway was built, opening in 1824.

Regrettably the Dinorwig Railway was no great shakes. The original diggings were centred near what became Alltwen and Alltdu quarries circa SH591611 where the inclines had been sited to lower material to Llyn Padarn. Work was now progressing southeast at the same level developing into what became Dinorwig quarry proper. It would have been logical to continue to use the inclines and run the rails along the edge of the lake, particularly since new work was migrating downwards Unfortunately this way was blocked by Fachwen quarry SN578615 where neither landowner Lord Newborough nor tenant Edward Shelton had reason to do Assheton-Smith any favours. Consequently the line that started at what came to be called Mills Level was laid alongside the 1812 road. The necessity to up-haul product from the newer workings to reach it seems to have been acccpted because sawing and reduction was concentrated at this level.

After passing through Dinorwig village, the railway left

the road at SH578628 and plunged straight down to Clwt y Bont below Deiniolen via the two-pitch Cwm incline. The line then continued for some 3 miles, almost level but with some slight against-the-load gradients before dropping down to the port by way of the Garth incline at SH550680. Unlike the Penrhyn layout that had 3 inclines approximately equally spaced, the Dinorwig line with a double incline close to one end and a single near the other end was more difficult to operate. Apart from the lack of handling room between the two pitches of the Cwm inclines, having two short and one long haulage stretches caused delays. Besides this, some of the earthworks were skimped and the slate sleepers broke. Horses used at either end were respectively stabled at the quarry and the port, and those used on the between inclines section were stabled at an ostlery depot at the foot of the lower Cwm incline.

A big water powered writing-slate works was opened alongside the line at Clwt y Bont SH561632. Curiously it not only outlasted the line by the better part of a century, but also prospered eventually occupying a second site powered by the original site's tail race and a third site also water powered at SH580633 in Deiniolen village. En-village sites were often chosen not just for the availability of water, but also to offer close to home employment for older and disabled men and also women whose presence on a quarrying site was unwelcome even well into the 20th century. Both the Clwt y Bont sites survived as engineering works, while the third became the headquarters of the Deiniolen Band. There was a line-side shoeing smithy at Rhydau SH565656 and this outlasted the line's closure by a full 100 years and still exists rebuilt as a dwelling. In addition, apart from a few relatively minor diversions, modern roads still define the line's route.

It soon became apparent that this Dinorwig Railway would not do and a new line was planned to run some 300' above the lake to pass behind Fachwen but although some earthworks were started the broken nature of the ground below Deiniolen caused this route to be abandoned. Since by now Shelton had transferred his affections to Glynrhonwy Quarry SH565607 on the other side of the valley and wanted to be rid of the Fachwen lease and even wealthy Lord Newborough could not refuse Assheton-Smith's offer of £13,500 for land that his grandfather had bought for £500, the way was open to run the line from the lowest point of the quarry along the north side of the lake through Fachwen land (Re-named Vaynol). By now Thomas Assheton-Smith (snr) had died and his much more modern-minded son was in full command, so applying 'Cutting-edge' technology the new line was planned for steam locomotion. This was a most bold decision since due to their appetite for fuel; industrial locomotives were virtually confined to coalfield use. The engineer appointed to design the line was James Spooner who had just completed the Ffestiniog Railway. Although in a couple of decades time the FR would prove that steam could be applied to quarry gauge locomotives, in the late 1830s this was not the case. The state of steam engine expertise at the time dictated a minimum gauge of 4' and also precluded any appreciable gradients. Taking up Dadford's original Penrhyn idea of carrying quarry wagons pic-a-back, the 4' gauge trucks would each carry 4 quarry wagons (except for the last in a rake that carried 3 plus a 'sentry-box' guard's cabin) from the quarry to Penscoins above Porth Dinorwig assisted by a with-the-load gradient of 1 in 230. At Penscoins the quarry wagons would be crewled four at a time, down an incline to the harbour. This head of incline area became a depot in itself with workers' housing, an engine and later a carriage shed and the drum house SH741678 (sadly destroyed by the Porth Dinorwig bypass) besides serving its primary purpose provided shelter for the handling the quarry wagons on and off the transporter trucks. In its initial form the quarry wagons were attached to an endless chain, on under-floor sheaves this arrangement being replaced in the late 19th century by a conventional overhead drum.

The line was completed in 1843 although locomotive working did not begin for another 5 years but when it was, Assheton-Smith must have thought "Eat your heart out Ted" - Edward Gordon Douglas, later Baron Penrhyn of the Second Creation who with a southwesterly wind would have been able to hear the engine's whistles from his much despised castle. Although other slate railways have survived as tourist lines, the Padarn railway hauled slate by steam for a record 113 years. Oddly, although both the Ffestiniog and the Penrhyn railways ran workmen's trains as soon as they were steamed, up to 1895 the only passengers on the Padarn were the proprietors, the most senior officials and VIP guests.

Porth Dinorwig became more than just a port and industrial settlement, being a virtual town in its own right its population of over 2000, greatly outshining Porth Penrhyn and even having in 1894, its own cattle market. A generator house on the quayside supplied electricity to the whole settlement, one of the earliest public supplies in the world, although the 1853 gas works continued to light the streets.

Ships had been built in the vicinity in the early 19th century and possibly before, but shipbuilding at Porth Dinorwig itself started in 1849 when Rees Jones re-located from Barmouth. Although ships could be built on any piece of flat, water-adjacent ground Rees Jones' yard was the full works, employing 30 permanent tradesmen and possibly double this number when work demanded. It was virtually self-sufficient even having its own sail loft. By the time he and his son completed their last vessel, the 80-ton schooner *F K Musprat* in 1894 they had built almost 30 vessels, for much of that time making a launch every year. Very few were under around 100 tons and during the 1860s when orders tapered off, sizes increased to 2-300 tons and included brigs. One of their last ships, the Barque *Ordovic* of 1878 was at 875 tons the largest ship ever built in north Wales.

Local ships were largely locally crewed and often locally owned. Thomas Turner the Dinorwig Agent the son of William Turner, being one local owner but tradesmen and professional men took shares in ships and the shipbuilding Jones family had an interest in a number of vessels. Like Penrhyn, as wood and sail gave way to iron and steam, the Dinorwig Quarry built up a fleet of up to half a dozen iron steamers one, the Vaynol was claimed to be the first ship to enter the Manchester Ship Canal when it opened in 1891 (carrying slate, of course!) The Dinorwig fleet was managed by Duff, Herbert and Mitchell Ltd who also ran the ship repairs at Porth Dinorwig. Their last vessel the *Juliet Duff* was not sold until the mid 1950s. There were several other 'lines' based mostly having just a single vessel but the Eryri Shipping Company a Llanberis-based partnership that included the local chemist, had 4 ships amply justifying such a title.

With the increasing demand for coal for the quarry, the railway, industry, the limekiln and increasingly domestic use, many ships arriving to load slate carried coal, others came in ballasted with stone which accounts for the 'alien' stone manifest in buildings in Porth Dinorwig. The port also handled general cargo including goods for the shops that like so many in Welsh coastal towns would have obtained supplies by sea from Liverpool merchants by the regular coastal steamers that remained competitive with rail right up to and even beyond WW2.

Motor lorries were freely available post WW1, but until the liberalisation of speed limits in the 1950s they were too slow for long distance deliveries. Hence Porth Dinorwig like similar harbours around the coast had regular sailings to ports around Liverpool Bay and beyond, tradition and low fares enabling them to defy railway competition.

In 1852 as was the case at Porth Penrhyn, the London and North Western Railway ran a sub-branch into Porth Dinorwig, giving it the distinction of having tracks of 3 different gauges, the 24½" gauge for the quarry trucks sent down the incline, the standard gauge and the 8' gauge of the mobile crane. Since so much of their output went overseas rail connection had a lesser impact on shipping than at Porth Penrhyn but later an increasing tonnage was sent by rail for loading at ports such as Liverpool to be shipped on large ocean-going steamers.

The railway link provided an additional incentive to the development of a foundry, engineering shops and two slate manufacturing works. Although space was found for a considerable enlargement of port facilities by the construction of a completely new dock (The 1858 Outer Harbour), space (and water for power) would remain a problem. Consequently in the 1880s a major independently owned slate works complex was established at Pont Rhythallt where it could be powered by the river Seiont. One works, Pont Rhythallt SH540641 produced a variety of slab products, the other Crawia SH536643 produced writing slates. Occupying a narrow site some ¼ mile long between the Padarn railway and the L&NWR Llanberis branch it had a choice both of slate supply and of dispatch route for finished products.

What was in effect a further expansion was made across the Menai strait at Pwllfanogl SH530709 where the splendidly named Welsh Imperial School Slate Factory (Britannia Works). It had its own port facility where timber for the frames could be landed as well as slate from Porth Dinorwig or Porth Penrhyn and coal for its two steam engines. Dispatch could be made by water but most was carted to Llanfair PG

45

station. There was also a further putative Anglesey development at Trefarthen SH490665 on Faenol land where slate was dug and shipped across the Straits at Moel y Don.

As at Porth Penrhyn most commercial matters relating to the quarry were attended to at an office at the port but the star in the Porth Dinorwig firmament was the dry dock. Flourishing well into the steam and steel era, it had an especial reputation for the maintenance of steam yachts dating from the time when Thomas Assheton-Smith II kept his steam yacht there. Right up to WW2 it was where the industrialists and shipping magnates of Liverpool and Manchester brought their steam yachts for maintenance and winter lay-up. Thanks to having the only dry dock on the north Wales mainland, Porth Dinorwig survived as an independent engineering and ship repair centre for several years after the quarry closed, under the guidance of 'Smith' as David Smith the formidable general foreman was known to all.

Dinorwig's manpower plus that of the independent quarries totalled about 3000 creating housing problems. Until the opening of the Padarn Railway extended the travel opportunities most Dinorwig quarry workers lived in Dinorwig, Deiniolen and in several chapel-nucleated settlements as well as tiny disparate cottages and smallholdings, mainly on the northeastern side of the valley. Many lived in Llanberis which in the late 18th century had not even been a hamlet, predominantly they were supervisors and middle management or workers in the independent quarries, with others of these latter living in Cwm-y-glo and Nant Perris. Immediately the Padarn line opened, being almost level it was practicable for workers to live at say Penllyn, Pontrhyhallt, Llanrug and Bethel, or even Porth Dinorwig and travel daily to work not by workmen's trains that were not introduced until 1895 but by hand or pedal-powered 'Velocipedes'. Some weekly barrackers came from as far away as Brynsiecyn on Anglesey. They in pre-train days had to do their pedalling having got up at 3 am to walk to Moel y Don, endured the ferry and climbed the port incline. When the trains started at least they could rest for the last part of the journey although they might still have to climb many hundreds of feet to their workplaces. In 1947 when the barracks closed a daily bus service got them home in half an hour!

Paradoxically the Padarn Railway bold, innovative and pioneering though it was gradually became a burden in latter days. Its carrying of quarry wagons on transporter trucks so avidly copied, became a handicap as did the unloading and crewling of wagons on the port incline. In addition underused locos had to be kept in steam at the port to handle quarry wagons The 1870s steaming of the Penrhyn Railway made the Padarn look like a very sick dinosaur. Despite this it was kept in use for a full 40 years after other slate producers had begun to depend on the motor lorry. Yet in another paradox when, in the 1930s a totally fresh opening was made by the Dinorwig Company at Marchlyn SH602628 in what proved to be an unsuccessful attempt to work their veins from a new direction, there was no thought of rail connection.

Both the Padarn Railway and the main line railway link to the port were closed in 1961 (workmen's trains being replaced by buses in 1947) and the port's last shipment of slates (from Penrhyn!) was in 1962. The whole port area is now a housing estate and marina.

# 4

# CAERNARFON

The third area in the northwest of Caernarfonshire where slate was successfully won was on the wastelands of Cefn Ddu (to the south of Llanberis), and on Moel Tryfan (to the southeast of Caernarfon) and on the northern flank of the Nantlle valley. There were a number of independent diggers working rock much of which allowed them not only to produce slates in larger and hence more expensive sizes than elsewhere but also slates that were thinner and hence cost less to transport and allowed lighter roof timbering. Moreover a large proportion of their out turn could be classed as 'Bests' By the latter part of the 18th century they had built up a substantial trade with Ireland, much at Penrhyn's expense. It was an important market since unlike today when only some 10% of the population of the British Isles lives in Ireland, and then the proportion was nearer 30%. Dublin was then not only a fast-expanding city, but also a prosperous one prepared to pay the premium price that their product commanded. In addition shipments to Ireland were not subject to the coastwise tax levied from 1794 on cargoes to say Liverpool and when shipments could be made at Forydd a little creek at SH484589 port tolls were avoided.

More importantly they operated on Crown land that Sir John Wynn of Glynllifon had rented in the mid-18th century but disputes over the lease between Sir John's son, Lord Newborough and the Crown agent, resulted in royalties being paid to neither. All in all this added up to a very profitable package indeed for the diggers.

*Course of original 1801 Penrhyn Railroad at Llandegai (Author's collection)*

*Bont Fawr, Nantlle Railway c1980 (Author's collection)*

*Dinorwig wagons on transporter truck, Padarn Railway*
*(By kind permission National Library of Wales)*

*Padarn Railway 'Velocipede' at National Slate Museum (Author's collection)*

*Gorseddau Railway trackbed, Porthmadog (Author's collection)*

*Blaenycwm extension Gorseddau Junction & Portmadoc Rly (Author's collection)*

51

*Croesor Tramway wrecked trucks at foot of Rhosydd incline (Author's collecion)*

*Croesor Tramway bridge (Author's collection)*

*Ffestiniog Railway* Little Wonder *at Harbour Station*
*(by kind permission National Library of Wales)*

*Ffestiniog Railway, train at Penrhyndeudraeth crossing (Author's collection)*

*Rhiw-bach Tramway 1900s (Courtesy of the late Mr G. R. Jones MA)*

*Rhiw-bach Tramway formation c1990 (Author's collection)*

*Ffestiniog & Blaenau Railway, train on Manod Viaduct*
*(By kind permission National Library of Wales)*

*Hafod y Llan Tramway formation (Author's collection)*

*Corris Railway crossing Dyfi Bridge*
*(By kind permission Nationl Library of Wales)*

*Dinas Mawddwy Railway terminus c1900 Locomotive is* Mawddwy
*(Courtesy Mr David Bates)*

*Tal-y-llyn Railway, Wharf station (Author's collection)*

*Slate quay on river Teifi, Fforest nr Cardigan (Author's collection)*

*Deeside Tramway, children help to return empty trucks on a
Summer morning 1930s (Courtesy Mr R. M. Williams)*

*Glyn Valley Tramway, mixed passenger and slate train
(By kind permission National Library of Wales)*

*Conwy Ferry at Tal-y-cafn (By kind permission National Library of Wales)*

*Gwen 154-ton schooner built at Conwy in 1866 probably by Richard Roberts*

*Porth Penrhyn 1900s*

*Porth Dinorwig 1900s? (By kind permission National Library of Wales)*

*Slate quays Caernarfon*

*Griffith Owen's yard, Nefyn 1880. On the stocks 107-ton schooner* Venus, *the last ship to be built at Nefyn*

61

Koh-i-noor *a 150-ton Barque built at Pwllheli 1852*

Edwin *a 159-ton topsail schooner built by David Williams at Pwllheli in 1852*

Gestiana *98-ton 3-masted schooner the last Porthmadog build launched from David Williams' yard in 1913*

*Porthmadog Harbour 1904. David Jones and David Williams were still building to the left of picture, where Ebenezer Roberts built up the 1890s. The ship on the right is laying at Greaves Wharf, the site of Henry Jones' yard.*

*R. J. Owens, 97-ton 3-masted schooner (Western Ocean Yacht) being built at Rotten Tare, Porthmadog, in 1907 David Williams, the builder extreme right. The close-spaced ribs are typical of Porthmadog ships.*

*Aberdyfi c1900 (By kind permission National Library of Wales)*

*'Borth y Gest. Site of Richard Jones' yard in distance on right.'*

The Acts of Union of 1801 reinforced the economic ties with Ireland but also reminded others of the importance of this market. In 1802 with trade picking up, this situation seemed a great business opportunity to four Caernarfon men. Much to the chagrin of Lord Newborough they obtained a lease from the Crown and formed the Cilgwyn and Cefn Ddu Company. With the intention of creating a "New Penrhyn", the syndicate offered the diggers the choice of leaving or paying royalties. Neither option appealed to these independently minded men and since bailiff bamboozling was second nature to them, the Company's revenues were thin. Despite taking on other less contentious sites and enjoying a measure of prosperity up to the early 1820s, dissidence amongst the partners caused the outfit to lapse into obscurity.

Whilst the Cefn Du workings rather languished, things went ahead in the Cilgwyn/Nantlle area with companies formed to take over and develop various diggings. Besides Cilgwyn itself at SH541540, Cloddfa Coed SH493532, Pen y Bryn SH50553 and Tal-y-sarn SH495435, together with several smaller units were by 1820 overwhelming the limited facilities at Forydd. Thus increasing tonnages were being carted to Caernarfon but cartage costs and turnpike tolls were eating into profits.

The Penrhyn Railway had demonstrated how dramatically rails could reduce costs but with diverse ownership of the quarries, the ground they occupied and of the land between them and the coast, a Penrhyn style link seemed out of the question, anyway Dinorwig was managing fine without one.

The opening of the Dinorwig line in 1824 was a wake up call that reducing transport costs had to be taken seriously.

The four major quarries got together to build what would become the Nantlle Railway. It was decided from the start that to be viable it would have to be open to all comers and operated as a turnpike, users paying a toll for running their own wagons and horses on the line. Edge rails would not be used, instead the now rather passé tram plates would be laid in the belief that this would facilitate its use by carts and even gentlemen's carriages In fact although tram plates had been bought, when the line opened in 1826 it had edge rails and of 3' 6" gauge to give a truck size more practicable for general use than the approximately 2' used at the two existing quarry rail lines. The route ran from amidst the quarries on the north side of the Nantlle valley, to the Caernarfon Slate Quays tight under the castle's walls. There was a minimum of civil work, apart from one short tunnel under the Coed Helen estate, a bridge over the Seiont and another over the Gwyrfai, it was almost a matter of just laying rails on the ground. There were no gradients and of course no inclines. The comparatively wide gauge proved less of a disadvantage than might be thought; movement within the quarries of rubbish and raw block was handled on 2' gauge tracks, while finished product was dispatched in 3'6" gauge wagons. There was also some use made of wagons having loose-on-axle, double-flanged wheels to enable then to run on both gauges.

The railway encouraged the opening of many new diggings, some of which due to landowners trying to maximise returns, were on setts too small to be viable and creating the malaise that chronically dogged the Nantlle valley – lack of tipping space. Despite this, Penyrorsedd SH509539 and Dorothea SH500532, became among the largest and certainly the longest lasting in the valley. Dorothea's success was not immediate and when the first operator failed to pay wages the employees demonstrated that the men in these parts were not ones to tangle with by burning down his house!

This Nantlle Railway was innovative in several ways, it was the first slate railway not owned by a single quarry and not running over the quarry landlord's own ground, it was open for public use and shortly would also carry passengers – all very novel indeed. The concept of mineral rolling stock being the property of the user later became commonplace (e.g. in the coal trade) and there were later similar instances of passenger stock also (Pullman cars). However the concept of the whole train including motive power being independently operated has only recently been copied (not always happily). A vital difference between the Nantlle and the other two slate lines was the fact that it terminated not only at a commodious and long established public harbour, but that that harbour was backed by a large town with not only a long seafaring tradition but also with a valuable infrastructure of trades and professions.

Caernarfon had been established on the estuary of the river Seiont by the Romans to supply their garrisons by sea safe from depredations by the indigenous tribes. Similarly Edward I sited the pivotal castle of his chain erected to subdue (or attempt to subdue) the local lads who had firmly-held views on subjugation. In more settled times the impractabilities of land travel meant that the port of Caernarfon remained the commercial capital of north-western Wales. The opening of Telford's road and the laying of railways in the early and the mid 19th century respectively increased the importance of Bangor.

Despite all north Caernarfonshire slate being described as 'Bangor', Caernarfon still retained its pre-eminence. Slate works proliferated in the town and included at various times– Humphreys Castle Works, Owen Roberts, Richard Evans, Griffiths and Williams, Richard Owen, Thomas Owen and James Owen, John Jones and Owen Jones, Nicholas and Owen and Fletcher that later amalgamated with Dixon to run the Victoria docks slate works until the 1980s and as Fletcher Dixon were with Gordon Richards prominent in Caernarfon slate manufacture and merchanting for much of the 20th century. Despite the local Cambrian Series slate being vulnerable to the thermal shock of the process, John Jones, Nicholas and Owen and probably others had enamelling kilns.

Despite there being slate works on almost every street, Caernarfon's greatest reputation was as a centre of excellence for engineering. Owen Thomas' foundry on the slate quays became De Winton's, a works that produced a wide variety of quarrying equipment, were pioneers in the building of marine steam engines and a prolific producer of the De Winton 'Coffee Pot' locomotives that were almost universal on industrial light railways. Humphrey Owen & Sons besides running the Vulcan Foundry also had a big timber yard. D. J. Williams, Brunswick Iron Works was regarded as one of the premier fine ironworkers in Britain and it was they who in 1919 produced at short notice the handles for the coffin of the Unknown Soldier.

Several of these engineering and slate establishments were on the Slate Quay on the north bank of the river close to the castle walls, which was where the Nantlle Railway terminated and had its offices. Most slate quarries in the Llanberis, Cwm Gwyrfai and Nantlle area had offices in the town, even the Prince of Wales quarry SH549498 when it was still a tiny scratching carting out through Cwm Gwyrfai, maintained an office at Caernarfon. One of more bizarre offices was that of Mr Webb the quarry explosives supplier, whose premises alongside County Hall were raided by the police following the 1869 tragic explosion at Cwm-y-glo, it being found that he was keeping 'samples' of nitro-glycerine in his office. In 1875 the opening of the Victoria dock with its 'Patent' slip and its rail connection from the railway station boded well for Caernarfon's ambitions to match and surpass Porthmadog, but the additional prosperity it brought was short lived since only 3 years later the slate trade collapsed.

68

Although ships have been built at Caernarfon since at least the early 14th century, the town's importance as a shipbuilding centre is not always apparent. From 1758 to the end of the 18th century around 40 vessels were built mostly small sloops but several were over 100 tons including 2 brigs. By the early 19th century launches averaged 5 per year, most being sloops for coastal work and would have helped to meet the burgeoning demand at Porth Penrhyn and Porth Dinorwig. From then until 1870 the build rate settled down to a couple per year with the predominance of schooners and the occasional brig reflecting increased voyage lengths. Activity tapered off in the 1870s effectively ending in the early 1880s with just one 17-ton smack, *Idris* being completed in 1898. During the 19th century almost 200 ships wee built, originally being laid down along the east bank of the Seiont, but as the slate merchants hijacked this waterfront space, shipyards migrated to what became the Victoria Dock. Over the years there were numerous builders, many of whom may have only built a single ship and records suggest that only 3 builders reached double figures, Thomas Williams (c28), William Jones (c16) and Owen Barlow (10) with Jones being the most productive since he was only in business for 8 years.

The pressure on water frontage explains why so much shipbuilding occurred at numerous inauspicious creeks, despite lacking the support of forges, sawmills and sail and rope makers available at a large port such as Caernarfon. Occasional builds took place at a number of places along the coast of Llŷn, most vessels were small sloops or schooners but in 1874 Llanealhaern launched *Ior*, a Barquentine of 230 tons. More substantial was Porth Dinllaen that in the course of 100 years up to 1876 turned out almost 60 vessels more than a dozen including two brigs of over 100 tons, these large vessels meant that this little port launched a bigger aggregate tonnage than Bangor. Nefyn in the same period turned out well over a hundred, almost all were sloops and schooners and while some were small, in the latter decades most were around 100 tons and *Isolina* of 1866 was a 290-tonner. Some of these north Llŷn builds were engaged in the granite and other trades but most augmented the ever-expanding slate fleets.

Ship owning was as at other port towns originally a matter for long-pocketed landowners, gradually filtering down though the professional classes to quite modest persons, in addition folk such as the Darbishires, owners of the Penyrorsedd quarry, foundry man J. P. De Winton and businessman and benefactor Sir Llywelyn Turner, son of William Turner of Blaenau Ffestiniog and Dinorwig, all of whom entered ship owning as an extension of their primary activities.

As was usual in seaports, retired captains, or their widows gave classes in navigation, but in Caernarfon there was one unusual teacher, Ellen Edwards whose father Captain Francis taught at Amlwch for many years. She followed her father's occupation but with the decline of Amlwch shipping set up in Caernarfon where she taught every aspect of seamanship for over 50 years some of the most notable mariners of her day. Amongst her alumnae were many famous masters in sail and steam including John Pritchard, first master of *Mauritania*. On her retirement she was uniquely granted a pension by Queen Victoria.

The Nantlle Railway after it was extended eastwards to Penyrorsedd served all the quarries on the north side of the Nantlle valley. A branch served some of the smaller quarries to the south and all went (almost) happily for nearly 40 years until 1866 when Thomas Savin extended the Bangor – Caernarfon Railway south from its Caernarfon terminus by tunnelling under the town. He had hoped to tap the rocky riches of Blaenau Ffestiniog but had to be content with connection to the Cambrian Railways at Afon Wen allowing him a most roundabout access to Porthmadog. Having bought the Nantlle Railway he, with scant regard for the users, laid his rails on much of its track bed as far as Pen-y-groes. This meant that the Nantlle wagons could only run as far as Tyddyn Bengam near Pen-y-groes, where they were pick-a-backed three at a time onto standard gauge trucks and off loaded at Coed Helen to be sent along the river bank to the Slate Wharf on the then still extant Nantlle rails. Later the Nantlle was further subsumed by a sub branch to Tal-y-sarn, where slate was loaded into standard gauge trucks which with Nantlle metal having been replaced on the Slate Quays with standard gauge track and traversers, enabled ships to be loaded direct from standard gauge trucks. On the other hand the traffic could by-pass Caernarfon and continue either to Deganwy where they could ship free of port dues, or stay on rail for delivery to British users.

Although terminating at Tal-y-sarn, emasculated to a length measured in yards, the Nantlle Railway bucked the trend and defeated the odds to become almost the last surviving slate railway, the sole horse-drawn stretch of the British Railways network. When it closed in 1963 it was probably the only section not losing money.

As happened on the Padarn Railway, independent slate processors set up adjacent to the line, David Roberts at Pen-y-groes SH469533 and Robert Griffiths a little distance off at Llanwnda SH474585, but spectacularly more successful was the Tudor slate works of Inigo Jones at Groeslon SH470551. Originally opened as a writing slate factory, it re-invented itself as an enamelling works. Unfortunately the Nantlle slate proved less than ideal for enamelling and more suitable slate had to be sourced in central Wales, successively buying Cae'r Defaid SH744285 and Cymerau SH777107 to ensure continuity of supply. A curious sequel is that it continues to flourish as a high-class slab products producer in common ownership with Aberllefenni mill SH768103 adjacent to Cwmerau.

Following the demise of the Cilgwyn and Cefn Du Company almost a dozen quarries were working the old partnership diggings on the slopes of Cefn Du facing Dinorwig on the south side of Llyn Padarn. In fact the potential was beginning to attract the attention of investors such as Shelton (late of Fachwen). But since the Padarn Railway was on the wrong side of the lake and both it and the Port were strictly reserved for Dinorwig quarry, they could only look enviously across Llyn Padarn as trainloads of slate merrily chugged to Porth Dinorwig, while they laboriously carted to Caernarfon.

Those near the summit used the present mountain road down to Waun Fawr, whilst those lower down used the Castel Bryn Bras road to Llanrug. Better, but not that much better than the time when diggers at what became Glynrhonwy Quarry Lower SN565607 would take blocks by boat to split into slates at their homes at Cwm-y-glo. (Literally a cottage industry?) By mid-century when it had become a flourishing enterprise Glynrhonwy Lower replaced their horses with a traction engine, but they acquired some unpopularity when it ran away down the slope to the Slate Quays and assaulted the castle.

Everything dramatically changed for the area when Savin's Afon-wen extension from Caernarfon having brought the standard gauge to the south of the town, provided an opportunity to lay a line up the Seiont valley to Llanberis. Although tunnelling was avoided, topography and land ownership forced crossings and re-crossings of the river calling for seven bridges in half a dozen miles. Following the river as it did, it could eventually serve river-powered industries such as the cluster of industries (Including slate working) at Peblig SH512631, the Seiont brickworks and Griffith Roberts' Glanmorfa writing slate factory SH 484614 just outside Caernarfon.

The line opened in 1869, the immediate beneficiary being Glynrhonwy Lower through whose yard the line actually ran enabling it and Glynrhonwy Upper SH560606 direct siding access. Goodman's quarry SH573606 at the other end of the quarrying area was able to build a tramway to Llanberis station, but the quarries in between high on the mountainside were left in remote isolation.

This was solved by the building of the mighty and ultimately 4-pitch, Ffridd incline system that eventually allowed every other working of consequence access to an exchange siding at the lakeside. The 1000-yard lower pitch was too long for gravity working so empties had to be raised by steam engine. The shorter upper pitches were gravity worked in the usual manner. Several of the workings that lay at anything up to 1200' above the railway became substantial undertakings.

The railway gave these independents a decade of absolute bonanza until the late 1870s recession, but even so thanks to this line, some workings survived into the interwar years. At first the slate destined for sea-carriage was put aboard at Deganwy, but the re-gauging of the tracks at the Caernarfon Slate Quays enabled some to be shipped at Caernarfon although an increasing proportion remained on rail. This line's brief heyday suggests that it is doubtful if it ever recovered its construction costs, nevertheless helped by the creation of the Snowdon Railway it enabled Llanberis to become a major tourist centre. This Llanberis branch played an important part in WW2. It facilitated the use of Glynrhonwy's mills area for important war production and of the establishment of R A F Llanberis, which was the main bomb depot for Bomber Command, safe from enemy air raids.

It also enabled the Daimler Company to move their aero-engine production machinery to Peblig Mill when their Coventry factory was bombed.

By the early 1870s the demand for slate had become a stampede yet lack of transport meant that quarries in areas such as the Cwm Gwyrfai and the slate-rich windswept heights of Moel Tryfan were missing out. Admittedly Braich quarry SH510552 and Fron quarry SH515548 had the John Robinson Tramway, but this creaking little line only took wagons to the top of Cilgwyn quarry from where they had to be crewled down a series of inclines to the Nantlle Railway – in itself fast becoming anachronistic.

Like a White Knight riding to a maiden's rescue, came the General Undertaking of the North Wales Narrow Gauge Railways. Happily the name was shortened, but then so was the scheme. The original plan included a narrow-gauge route from Caernarfon to Porthmadog, via Beddgelert with a branch off from there that would have taken in Betws-y-coed and even Corwen (that just for starters). In the end it only got as far as Rhyd-ddu a barren, wind-scoured waste where slate pickings were scant but the opportunities for conveying Snowdon-bound excursionists were abundant, or would have been had the summit railway planned to start from there, not been built at Llanberis on the other side of the mountain. More seriously, it had been assumed that the London and North Western Railway who now owned Savin's Afon-wen line would either make land available to enable them to reach Caernarfon or would third rail its track from Dinas to Caernarfon. Unsurprisingly these assumptions proved incorrect so the NWNGR had to terminate at the L&NWR station at Dinas, where slate would be transferred into standard gauge wagons for carriage to Caernarfon. In addition, the line was not fully open, or as fully open as is was going to get until 1881, at the start of the bleakest decade in the slate trade for half a century.

Curiously this 'half a railway' with which the NWNGR finished up was only completed by bamboozling quarry users to bankroll it. On its main line several quarries had connections but only Glanrafon SH581540, Hafod y Wern SH530571 and possibly Clogwyn y Gwin 576530, produced anything more than nominal tonnages. Bwlch Cwmllan SH600521 and Llyn y Gadair SH564519 planned but never built rail connections. However the Bryngwyn branch opened up for the first time the virgin riches of Moel Tryfan. So at a time when slate quarries elsewhere were going bust on an almost daily basis, this one branch of a rather pathetic little railway teetering on the brink of bankruptcy; was creating some of the greatest slate success stories of the late 19th century. Cilgwyn quarry abandoned the uncertainties of the Nantlle and threw in its lot with the NWNGR. The tonnages coming from Cilgwyn, Alexandra quarry SH519562, Moeltryfan quarry SH515559 and neighbouring diggings only being limited by the capacity of the NWNG's Bryngwyn incline, which was incidentally the only incline on a locomotive-powered Welsh quarry railway.

After several abortive attempts the line eventually reached Porthmadog as the spectacularly unsuccessful Welsh Highland Railway of 1923, which carried almost no slate whatsoever on its main line. The quarries on the Bryngwyn branch kept it busy until 1933 when they found that they could reach the Railway (Now LMSR) at Pen-y-groes by motor lorry for a third of the cost. Its 21st century revival, which cocks a snook at the shades of the L&NWR by utilising their roadbed from Dinas to Caernarfon, has yet to prove its economic viability.

By the end of the third quarter of the 19th century Caernarfon had become a railway employer to rival Bangor. It had the Dinas exchange to add to the Llanberis branch and the Pen-y-groes junction for Tal-y-sarn, plus separate spurs to the riverside Slate Quays and the Victoria dock. The Victoria dock had considerably expanded Caernarfon's maritime capacity but the adage 'What goes on rail stays on rail' applied, this rail activity did little to benefit Caernarfon as a port. Material carried by the Nantlle Railway, the North Wales Narrow Gauge and the Llanberis branch all funnelled towards Caernarfon, but instead of finishing at the slate quays it dived through the town tunnel and proceeded on its merry way to England. Actually since Caernarfon's traditional markets were mostly in Britain its docks were bound to be more vulnerable to rail competition than ports with large overseas connections. Thus when the slate boom ended in the late 1870s each decade saw a halving of loadings at the Caernarfon quays and by the 1920s the port was actually handling slate imports.

Caernarfon apart, the pattern of settlement was mixed. Pen-y-groes, Tal-y-sarn, and to some extent Bontnewydd, Llanllyfni and Llanwnda grew into large villages housing, administering and supporting the quarry workforces, and even into the 1980s at these places shop hours and the general tenor of life still revolved around the dictates of the shift patterns of the long-gone quarries.

There were also a number of quarry-owned hamlets such as Nantlle and Rhyd-ddu and flourishing, chapel-nucleated settlements such as Carmel, Y Fron, Rhostryfan and Rhosgadfan. There were villages such as Pen-y-groes, Tal-y-sarn and Llanllyfni that were slate dependent. There are also many isolated dwellings with a patch of land where an animal or two and maybe crops raised, some on Crown land were allegedly *Tai Unnos* erected under the supposed rule that

76

houses built between sunset and sunrise automatically had good title.

Caernarfon slate wharves are now busier than they ever were – as a car park! The docks survive as a marina, but the maritime tradition is carried on by the Royal Yacht Club founded in 1847 by Sir Llywelyn Turner under the patronage of Queen Adelaide, widow of King William IV and with the 1st Marquis of Anglesey and Robert Stevenson as its first Commodore and Vice Commodore respectively. Acknowledged the premier yacht club of Wales it is headquartered in Porth yr Aur, the town's Watergate built in 1284 by Edward I.

5

# MAENTWROG and PORTHMADOG

The saga of the fleet of little boats carrying Blaenau Ffestiniog slate down afon Dwyryd from Maentwrog is so well known that it is sometimes forgotten that Maentwrog had been a port in its own right, for centuries the main shipping place for northern Merionnydd. It had a quay on the river immediately downstream of the bridge, another accessed by a canalised tributary and a third a little further off at Cemlyn. It handled the shipment of timber, wool and hides plus slates and the occasional gravestone from nearby Cae'n y Coed quarry SH681408, and it imported lime for the farmers and luxuries for the gentry.

Slate was dug near Llanffestiniog from at least the 16th century but purely for the convenience of the more affluent type of wool merchant or timber dealer. The notion that anyone would dig for slate at the head of the valley where just a few farmers attempted to survive in the harshest climate of any inhabited part of Wales; was unthinkable.

Famously Methusalem Jones a humble Cilgwyn slate digger guided by a dream walked to that very place in the early 1760s and struck his pick into a crag in the Diffwys Gorge revealing – 'Slate that scintillated like a jewel and glistened like a mountain lake'. The truth is that he was a man of some substance with a farm near Caernarfon and a pub in that town of which he later became a burgess. Possibly from gossip overheard in his pub he learned that good slate had already been found on Wern land at Bowydd farm, so he took a lease on the adjoining Gelli Farm, assembled some kind of syndicate and set about digging.

Thus in this most inauspicious location, described as God forsaken, but where in truth it seemed as if God had never been; dig they did, creating what became Diffwys quarry SH712463, the first commercial working of slate at what would become Blaenau Ffestiniog – slate that would ultimately be shipped to the proverbial 'Ends of the earth'.

Shipping it to the ends of the earth would prove easy compared with getting to the ship. The nearest navigable water was at Maentwrog, the road there from Llanffestiniog was not too trying but to get slate to Llan was a different matter entailing an arduous journey for most of the way in the panniers of an ass or a mule or any beast with a leg at each corner.

Just as difficult was selling the slate. Cargoes put aboard a ship would be either bought by the vessel's master or sold at a destination quay by the quarry's representative. Without any formal agency arrangements, this latter might call for someone from a quarry being on the spot and there is record of one Diffwys partner walking to London, meeting the boat. Selling the slate and walking back to Blaenau with the proceeds!

Reverting to the problems of carriage, by 1800 when Diffwys quarry was sold over the heads of the original partners to new owners (who included the redoubtable William Turner, later of Dinorwig) the Llan-Maentwrog road had been improved. The gradient had been eased and the present Tal-y-bont Bridge over the Cynfal had replaced the Pont Dôl Rhiw Felen, none of which of course helped getting slate to Llan. One of the first actions of the new owners was to build a road from the quarry to Tan y Manod and along line of the present main road to join just beyond Congl y Wal, a pre-existing road to Llanffestiniog. At the same time the digging on Bowydd farm that may have aroused Methuselah Jones' interest in the area, had been less than successful but the landowner, now Lord Newborough, seeing how well Diffwys was doing reopened this Bowydd working SH708464. Realising how poor access had contributed to its earlier failure, he built a road (now defined by a street) down through Four Crosses to pick up a pre-existing track over the river at Pont Fron Goch then on to Congl y Wal. (This route is still traceable as a lane).

In 1804 Manod quarry SH723452 that had opened up almost on the peak of Manod Mountain built its epic road from the quarry to join the Blaenau – Llan road (at some time later it was diverted to join the road from Penmachno down through Cwm Teigl. Apart from a few hundred yards near the halfway point, this magnificent track is still in good condition.

It would appear that there was no significant roadwork done for 15 years until Samuel Holland, having bought Rhibrifdir quarry SH 693473 built a road to join the pre-existing road that is now the main street of Blaenau Ffestiniog, to reach Four Crosses and join with Bowydd's traffic. For both Holland's and Bowydd's carts the climb up from Pont Fron Goch was a punishing one for the poor overburdened horses. In winter, it took the combined draught of two horses in tandem harness to move a mere half-ton (500Kg). Where the route levelled at Congol y Wal the lead horse could be unhitched and the load augmented a little from a roadside dump. Only at Llanffestiniog, could the load be made up to the cart's official one-ton capacity. Fortunately the climb was eliminated in the mid 1820s by a road being built (now the present main road) from Four Crosses to meet the Diffwys road at Tan y Manod.

Around 1830 it was all change again, when what is now the present road from Congol y Wal to Rhyd-y-sarn was built joining up with the road coming down from Cwmorthin, and on from Rhyd y Sarn by a pre-existing road (of sorts) to join with the Llanffestiniog road at Pont Tal-y-bont. These roads formed the basis of the Ffestiniog Turnpike Trust, which the increasing slate tonnage seemed to offer the prospect of being very profitable. Indeed it might well have been had not Samuel Holland on his way to the bank at Caernarfon, stopped at Pen-y-groes for a bar snack.

The Maentwrog quays were by now augmented by others further down river and the building and manning of the Dwyryd slate boats had become a substantial and efficient industry with both sides of the river providing the men and the boats. However with Blaenau outputs now exceeding those of Nantlle and matching those of Penrhyn and Dinorwig a railway was becoming a necessity. The plea that there was no port where such a railway could terminate was answered by the opening of a quay on ground reclaimed by the completion of the Cob embankment across the Glaslyn estuary and which was already dubbed Porthmadog. The Dwyryd boats were already trans-shipping there instead of at anchor at Ynysycyngar, and the Cob provided excellent access to this quay. As in the Nantlle case, building a railway was complicated by the diverse ownership of both land and quarries but here the terrain also posed engineering difficulties and there was dispute as to which route should be taken.

One route arose from Mr Rothschild having made Samuel Holland an offer he could not refuse for the Rhiwbrifdir quarry, had become the 'Mr Big' of Blaenau. Rothschild was in favour of a railway and had the funds to back one, the trouble was that he wanted it to serve not only Rhiwbrifdir but also to climb 1000 feet to run past his Moelwyn workings that perilously panniered their output by mountain track to the road at Rhyd. There was also a counter scheme to drop the line by inclines into the Vale of Maentwrog so that it could run along the Dwyryd and give users the option of loading onto the river boats or continuing to Porthmadog. Besides all this bickering about routes there was massive opposition to the whole idea of a railway, not only from the boatmen and the carters but also from the influential backers of the Turnpike Trust who saw their newfound income stream vanishing.

Thus we come to the famous 'Pie and a pint' (Probably a cup of tea and some bread and cheese!) chance meeting at Pen-y-groes between Holland who had by then started a new quarry at SH690466 above Rhiwbryfdir, and Irishman Henry Archer, who was contemplating acquiring the Nantlle Railway. Apparently Archer agreed to abandon interest in the Nantlle line and come to Blaenau and get a railway moving there. With Archer's ability to raise finance in Ireland, James Spooner engaged as engineer and the various objectors mollified, the Ffestiniog (or Festiniog as it then was) Railway opened in 1836.

It is impossible to overstate the engineering elegance of the FR. It was double the length of any other slate railway. Despite being on difficult terrain with a considerable difference in height between its termini it had no inclines, (other than the temporary haulage and gravity inclines over a hump pending the completion of the Moelwyn tunnel). Except for the last few hundred yards over the Cob the rakes of loaded wagons were totally gravity propelled, reaching speeds that made them probably the fastest vehicles on earth.

Oddly the support from the quarry proprietors was not immediate, Holland did not at first have direct connection for his Cesail quarry SH690466 due to an access dispute with Rothschild's Rhiwbryfdir, who although were themselves the first quarry to connect to the FR, did not do so for two years.

Lord Newborough having just completed Bowydd's magnificent Cei Newydd on the Dwyryd shunned the railway for a dozen years. Diffwys, one of the largest producers having sited Pant yr Ynn Mill SH709454 on its nice new road to take advantage of the power of the Du Bach stream continued to cart and boat until 1861. Manod (and adjoining Graig Ddu) quarries continued to use their road until 1866 when the Ffestiniog and Blaenau Railway gave them access to the FR. By which time Rhiw-bach SH740462 was able to abandon its difficult Cwm Teigl cartage when the eponymous tramway to Blaenau was opened. Braich Ddu SH718384 that had no practicable access to the FR continued to use boats until 1868 when the building of the Briwet Bridge obstructed navigation. When the Great Western Railway from Bala to Blaenau opened, Braich Ddu planned to lay a tramway to it but only got as far as the nearest public road.

Slate occurrences were not confined to Blaenau Ffestiniog itself, beyond the Moelwyns to the west is Cwm Croesor, a hanging valley that had become a dead-end when the Cob reclamation enabled the Dolgellau-Caernarfon road to by-pass it. There was slate there in comparative abundance, but finished product had to be laboriously pack-horsed. The FR might have been reached by cart at Tanygrisiau via Cwmorthin had not the Cwmorthin quarry SH681459 decided against doing favours to competitors and barred this route to wheeled vehicles. The opening of the Croesor tramway by the indefatigable H B Roberts in 1863 changed all that, giving access to Porthmadog to a number of quarries, especially Rhosydd SH664461, Croesor SH657457 and Pantmawr SH658466 who reached the tramway via spectacular inclines, and later by an equally spectacular tunnel.

The Croesor Tramway was a modest, horse-drawn affair that by means of three inclines lowered slate from half a dozen quarries down to the Cob-reclaimed land of the Glaslyn estuary, and on to Porthmadog. Although the lower, level section was utilised by the post WW1 Welsh Highland Railway, the elevated part was never steamed but quietly plodded on ignoring the vicissitudes of its busier neighbours. Even long after the tramway's official closure its trucks continued, hand pushed to serve the farmers as agricultural adjuncts and grocery-burdened housewives as 'shopping trolleys'.

Although trifling compared with the Ffestiniog Railway, the Croesor had an important advantage over it. When the Cambrian Railways line reached Porthmadog the line and station were on the landward side of the town, remote from the F.R., so Blaenau slate could not be transferred to the standard gauge, as was possible at say, Penrhyn and Dinorwig. The Croesor entered Porthmadog alongside an abortive Cambrian branch to Beddgelert, being used as a siding. Thus Croesor material could be readily loaded onto the Cambrian. Since the Croesor connected to the F.R. at the harbour, Ffestiniog traffic could reach the standard gauge, but only with difficulty. This town section of the Croesor incidentally also served to connect the great steam flourmill and the big manufacturing merchants and foundries to the harbour and the Cambrian.

The third slate rail line that converged on Porthmadog was the Gorseddau Tramway that although horse drawn was a little ambitious in its pretensions. It all started when some north-country men failed to realise that while the Blaenau veins extended into Cwm Croesor and further west, their quality and abundance tapered off beyond the Glaslyn. They eyed the remote fastnesses of Cwm Ystradllyn and decided that any geological difficulties could be sorted if enough money was thrown at it and that the failure to satisfactorily extract slate here was an indication of the lack of enterprise on the part of the native peasants. At Gorseddau quarry SH573453 it took them little time but a lot of money to find out how wrong they were. Their magnificent Ynys y Pandy mill SH550433 could be best described by paraphrasing Marshall Bosquet alleged comment on the charge of the Light Brigade at Balaclava 'C'est magnifique, mais ce n'est pas le slate'. To compound their folly they had also built their railway to Porthmadog to be also bigger and better - 3' gauge with formations and bridges to almost main line standard.

Ten years later another lot did much the same thing higher up Cwm Pennant at Prince of Wales quarry SH549498. They imagined that slate then being carried in trifling quantities on packhorses, could be expanded into a big industry by extending the Gorseddau line. They proceeded to build a vast quarry infrastructure, apparently confident that the use of the name of the errant heir apparent would guarantee success. They extended the line, renamed it the Gorseddau Junction and Portmadog Railway and re-laid the lot in 2' gauge metal to suit one of Mr De Winton's latest locomotives, the first of a fleet that would speed thousands of tons of slate and slate products to Porthmadog. In fact before long the entire output was just filling the occasional truck that was hand-pushed to Porthmadog. The further extension of the rails to an optimistically opened copper mine was even more unsuccessful.

The Porthmadog end of the line utilised the track bed of the Tremadog Tramway a disused ironstone line that itself utilised the embanked towpath of yet another transport route into Porthmadog, the Tremadog Canal, a short waterway cut to facilitate the supplying of Tremadog which proved to be more symbolic than practical. Its embankment undoubtedly is now busier in its present cycle track guise than it ever was in any of its previous roles. When one realises that the original

Tremadog Tramway used rails left over from the construction of the Cob and that in post-slate days part of the formation was used by a stone-carrying line from Moel y Gest, it is apparent that 'Recycling' is not a new concept.

In the meantime, of the three narrow gauge slate lines converging on Porthmadog, the Ffestiniog Railway was the only one to carry serious tonnages, but by the 1860s these tonnages had become onerous. With rakes of anything up to 100 loaded wagons plunging towards the port at alarming speeds with the tortured scream of the wheel flanges drowning out the protests and prayers of the brakeman clinging on as if his life depended on it (which of course it did), the capacity for carrying slate to Porthmadog was almost limitless. However horse-hauling back the empty wagons to Blaenau placed a definite limit on capacity. Particularly as fewer and fewer of the 'empties' were actually empty as the quarries' needs for coal, timber, gunpowder and engineering spares increased, not to speak of food, fuel, domestic supplies and beer and 'bacco for Blaenau Ffestiniog's burgeoning population. With hundreds of men working underground and thousands of households, Blaenau's weekly requirements for candles alone must have run into tons. Therefore the bold step was taken to emulate Dinorwig and steam the line.

Since locomotives climbing capabilities had been improved since the Padarn had been laid down, it was not necessary to change the trackbed, other than a short tunnel to avoid a rock-spur and by using Mr Fairlie's patent double locomotives; there was no call for re-gauging. Thus in 1863, almost overnight this industrial tramway became as much a legitimate goods (and passenger) line as any main line railway in the country.

The FR's slate traffic was augmented by the boot-lace zig-zags of the Moelwyn quarry SH661442 inclines, the suicidal swallow-dive of the Wrysgan quarry SH676458 incline and the Nyth y Gigfran SH689462 contribution almost vertically delivered. The Cwmorthin Tramway brought more traffic as did the Rhiw-bach Tramway which besides serving its namesake quarry opened up the workings to the east of Manod. In addition the (steamed) Ffestiniog and Blaenau Railway was fed by the great Graig Ddu inclines and indirectly from quarries in the Llanffestiniog area. These had no rail connection but one, Brynglas SH732423 had a short rail link to the Bala road and other Drum SH735431 had similar formations that were probably never railed.

Post-steaming, some 17 quarries could load their wagons and have them arrive at the Porthmadog quayside with their product pristine and unsullied.

The introduction of passenger services enabled the FR to be a true umbilical between the twin towns of Blaenau Ffestiniog and Porthmadog, but just as important was the opportunity it gave to work in Blaenau and to live outside this desperately overcrowded town in say Maentwrog, Penrhyn-deudraeth, Minfford or even Porthmadog without the trauma of weekly barracking. Although there were generally barracks attached to the larger quarries, most were overfull and so barracking in the Blaenau context might mean dossing in an outhouse or on a loft floor or even in a quarry building. Another effect was to emphasise that the centre of gravity of Blaenau had changed. Hitherto the official terminus of the FR had been at Dinas handy for the ex-Rothschild Welsh Slate Co, for Holland's Cesail, for Mathews's Gloddfa Ganol SH694470 and for Llechwedd SH700470, but with other quarries coming into the picture and the Dinas settlement which had once been the nucleus of Blaenau disappearing under a zillion tons of rubble, what had been the Dwffws branch became the main terminus and passenger station. This terminus that connected to two inclines from eight quarries was plumb in the centre of a vibrant amphitheatre of buildings clinging to a rock face that would have daunted a Snowdon goat, where pubs and chapels vied for supremacy in Montague/Capulet manner. Dominated by a contiguous horseshoe of quarries from Moelwyn to Manod, the town was devoted to slate.

Blaenau Ffestiniog was devoted to slate, Porthmadog was devoted to Blaenau Ffestiniog – they were industrial towns, the only truly industrial towns in northwest Wales two sides of the same coin as mutually interdependent as Siamese twins. Three quarters of a century before the Ffestiniog Railway united them, Blaenau Ffestiniog wasn't even a hamlet, less than a decade before; Porthmadog had not even been there.

Porthmadog was a full-scale port/town but unlike say Bangor or Caernarfon it had no reason to exist other than the supplying, maintenance and administration of slate quarries and the handling and processing of their products.

All the quarries in the region had offices in the town and most had carefully delineated sections of the quays to stock their product. There were solicitors, agents, accountants and banks to care for their interests but the great men of the town were the manufacturing merchants such as Richard Williams and Davies Brothers who set the prices and bankrolled the quarries. Just as notable were the foundries, Owen, Isaac and Owen of the Union Iron Works, the Glaslyn Foundry and the Britannia Foundry. None achieved the eminence of De Winton's of Caernarfon but they were able to capitalise on their reputations to obtain out of area orders after the decline of shipping and slate, Glaslyn and Britannia being both able to survive well into the post WW2 era.

There were pioneering Building Societies that helped to convert a marsh into a mini-city of over 5000 inhabitants. There were shops and traders of every kind, a steam flourmill and at neighbouring Tremadog a woollen mill with an international clientele.

Primarily, however Porthmadog was a port, a sailing ship port devoted to – the equipping of ships, the loading of ships, the manning of ships, the financing of ships, the repairing of ships – and the teaching of navigation and seamanship; but above all the building of ships. Aggregated with the overspill to Borth y Gest, between 1824 and 1913 more than 260 vessels were built at and mostly for, Porthmadog, which retained its sailing ship eminence well into the steam-ship era. This arose from the fact that whereas the Caernarfon slate ports chiefly dispatched coastwise, to Ireland and the near continent, Porthmadog dispatched worldwide. Early steamships were huge consumers of coal, so up to the late 19th century long voyages called for intermediate coaling stops, whereas of course a sailing ship had an almost unlimited non-stop capability. Steam freights were high, acceptable for urgent cargoes, which slate was not. In addition steam ship owners could not afford to have their vessels idle so could not accept the delay associated with the careful loading and stowing of slate.

Most ships were variations of the schooner fore-and-aft rig since they were more manoeuvrable in tight situations than square rigged ships and had the additional advantage that they could be sailed with a lower standard of Master's Certificate. Just as makers skew the design of medium sized commercial vehicles to enable them to be driven without an HGV licence, there was some ingenuity in the design of topsail schooners to provide a vessel with good before-the-wind performance that could still be sailed on a 'Fore-and-aft' ticket. Almost by accident this resulted in the late 19th century culmination of Porthmadog design, the 'Western Ocean Yachts'.

Long distance cargoes were not confined to slate. There is record of *Gomer* a 157 ton Snow built in 1821 at Traeth Bach on the lower Dwyryd, sailing for New York with 100 tons of slate carrying 94 emigrants (including women and children) and a crew of 9, all presumably bedding down in the hold, on the cargo!

*Gomer* was not of course a Porthmadog ship but one of a number built on Afon Glaslyn and afon Dwyryd to meet an increasing demand for vessels to accept the cargoes brought down the Dwyryd on the little slate sloops, long before Porthmadog became dry land. There is a record of the schooner *Aberkin* built at Talsarnau in 1786 being at St.Petersburg in 1795, and the relatively sizeable 121 ton Brig *Hawarden Castle* having been built at Traeth Mawr (Glaslyn estuary) in 1801 and in 1816 the 89-ton brigantine *Dauntless* being built there also. Traeth Bach (Dwyryd estuary) builds included the 128 ton *Eleanor* of 1812 and the *Unity* of 1813. Undoubtedly in addition to the river sloops, sea-going vessels were built on the Dwyryd as far up-river as Maentwrog. Similarly on the Glaslyn there would have been builds up to Aberglaslyn Bridge, including now land-locked places such as Prenteg and Llanfrothen.

Porthmadog shipbuilding probably can be dated from 1824 when the 64-ton smack *The Two Brothers*, the first recorded build of Henry Jones the great Porthmadog shipbuilder, quietly slid into the water from a green bank just across the river from where the present Harbour Station would be erected. At least 20 more vessels would follow her during the next ten years and more than double that number in the ensuing decade with the annual build rate increasing until 1856 when a ship per month was completed. The build rate eased afterwards but the average size of vessel increased thus in 1874 although there were only 5 completions total tonnage more than matched that of 1856. Ships fully laden with slate were crossing the bar outward bound under a full spread of sail within almost hours of being handed over.

The builders were pushed to find space to lay their keels since more and more of the harbour was annexed as stocking ground by the big quarries. With successive quarries claiming quay space culminating in Cwmorthin quarry having a quay almost in Borth y Gest, builders were badly squeezed and managed the best they could, not always amicably. Henry Jones was the most prolific builder but when he gave up in the late 1850s, having built over 40 ships his yard was usurped by J. W. Greaves of Llechwedd quarry. Builders had to resort to exiguous riverside places on the Dwyryd, doubtless employing the dispossessed builders of the Dwyryd sloops. The *Royal Charter* (Not the 2,700-ton steam/sail vessel so tragically lost off Anglesey, but a 119-ton schooner) was built at Abergafren near Minffordd in 1858. David Jones built the 107-ton schooner *Cynhaiarn* and the 186-ton barquentine *C. E. Spooner* in 1874 and 1878 respectively right up the Dwyryd at Cei Newydd prior to obtaining a yard near the FR Harbour Station near\r where quarry owner Sam Holland had first staked his claim to a piece of the quayside action. Nearby was the yard of veteran Ebenezer Roberts who gave up new builds in 1892 but alongside was David Williams' slip with whom Jones maintained and enhanced the Porthmadog tradition from the 1880s onwards.

All this called for a considerable body of support trades, the foundries took care of the iron fittings, winches etc, but obviously timber stockists were needed, as were sail, rope, spar and block makers. Chandlers too, able to supply besides candles, every on-board necessity from an oil lamp to a 'Donkey's Breakfast' (Straw mattress), to a chart of Chesapeake Bay, to a sou'wester hat. Obviously carpenters, blacksmiths and shipwrights were needed, as were dealers to supply them with tools, plus of course the schools of navigation that were part of every port.

The only seaport amenities notably lacking were of the less reputable variety, due possibly not so much to the vigilance of black befustianed chapel deacons as because most seamen were natives of the town with homes to go to and wives to welcome them.

It is often forgotten how important was marine insurance and what a pioneer in this was Porthmadog. The Portmadoc Mutual Insurance Society formed in 1841 being a model that other ports eagerly imitated. Although this venture was backed by Samuel Holland and other great Blaenau slate proprietors, insurance like ship owning was very much dependent on people of modest means. By the end of the 19th century insurance had become the province of the big Liverpool and London based Societies whose mindset was very much iron and steam based. Thus these local organisations still survived since they understood wood and sail and could judge the repute of local owners and masters.

By 1880 launching tonnage had reached a peak after which it took an abrupt dive, with only one vessel being completed between 1879 and 1890. There were several reasons for this, the Minffordd railway yard opened in 1872 offering extra stocking space, but more importantly it enabled slate coming down from Blaenau on the FR to be readily loaded directly onto the Cambrian Railways, before it even got near Porthmadog. The escalation of output was so great that the diversion of slate from sea to rail had at first been scarcely noticed at Porthmadog harbour, but 1874, well before the slate trade abruptly went sour, proved to be the peak year for Porthmadog slate shipments. Then in 1876 the LNWR arrived at Blaenau from Betws-y-coed, followed in 1882 by the Great Western reaching there from Bala, all meaning that increasing tonnages never went near Porthmadog. This move to rail not only affected home market consignments, but also with ocean-going steamers becoming longer ranged and larger, railway-borne slate was often going to Liverpool for shipment to Blaenau's traditional markets. In addition wooden sailing ships could be more cheaply obtained from say Prince Edward Island than from the local builders, and even ship owners who remained faithful to sail were ordering steel-hulled vessels from northeast England. Not only were the slipways vacant but also there was the inevitable domino effect among every trade and profession that supported shipbuilding.

There was some demand for ships during the 1890s not so much due to the temporary recovery in Blaenau's fortunes, as the paradoxical fact that orders were coming into the Porthmadog yards from the very part of world that was selling ships to Porthmadog. This was because the three-masted topsail schooners developed in Porthmadog in the yards of the rival builders David Jones and David Williams had a unique combination of handiness, speed and closeness of haul, with a strength of hull that bordered on indestructibil-ity; characteristics that endeared these 'Western Ocean Yachts' to the Canadian fish trade. However this market had its limitations so by the turn of the century launches had dropped to almost nominal figures. The last vessel was Gestiana, completed by David Williams in 1913 – as if to signal its anachronism, it was lost on its delivery voyage to its Newfoundland buyer.

From 1902 slate shipments declined rapidly and the grand scheme to make an impoundment on the landward side of the Cob that would have more than doubled the quay yardage, remained as an aspiration until 1914 when the loss of the German trade put an end to such ambitions.

Steamers were of course no strangers to Porthmadog - the

Carnarvonshire and Merionethshire Steamship Company had been formed in 1864, using *S. S. Rebecca* to carry stores from Liverpool to supply the growing town of Porthmadog. Replaced by *Rebecca II* in 1896, this latter and other ships continued these deliveries but were loading diminishing tonnages of slate.

The last locally built ships to trade out of Porthmadog, *David Morris* and *Elizabeth* departed in the 1920s but steamers and wooden vessels de-rigged and Diesel-engined continued to land general cargo and to pick up 2-3000 tons of slate per annum up to WW2. During the war supplies for and components from the war-work occupied foundries passed through the port. Although the F.R. closed in 1946, during the latter 20th century a few odd lorry loads of slate did find their way to the quays at Porthmadog, and some steamer-bourn supplies, including items for the construction of Trawsfynnydd power station, were landed on the slate wharves before they were 'marinaised'. The last vessel to regularly use Porthmadog is believed to be *Florence Cooke*, a vessel belonging to Cooke's Explosives of Penrhyndeudraeth whose cargoes were seriously unpopular with British Rail.

There was one last echo of the port's greatness in 2003 when a diving team found off the Georgia coast the wreck of the side-wheel steamer *Republic* lost on its way from New York to New Orleans in October 1865. Among its cargo were found Blaenau Ffestiniog writing slates, (possibly made in the Newborough mill). Although the frames had vanished the slates themselves were in perfect condition.

Now as at other ports Porthmadog's great maritime tradition rides on Museums, Marinas and rapidly fading Memories.

# 6

# PWLLHELI and MAWDDACH

## Pwllheli

The avalanche of slate that thundered down the Ffestiniog Railway from Blaenau Ffestiniog in the mid-19th century threatened Porthmadog with a Pompeian engulfment that could only be averted by having more and more and even more ships.

This need for ships in ever increasing numbers in ever increasing sizes capable of reaching increasingly distant lands began, thanks to the splendid efforts of the Dwyryd boatmen, long before Porthmadog emerged from the quicksands of Traeth Mawr. Even when the Porthmadog yards overran Borth y Gest, keel space could not be found to cope with the spiralling demand.

As a result many Porthmadog registered ships were built elsewhere Some at Caernarfon or Porth Dinorwig, some from Chester or Liverpool, the Bristol Channel, and even from the east coast of England, but rather inevitably from nearer at hand along the northern sweep of Cardigan Bay. To the west on Llŷn a good agricultural trade supported numerous ports such as Aberdaron, Abersoch and Rhiw, with of course castle-protected Cricieth operating on a larger scale. These ports had a history of seafaring and shipbuilding that enabled them, particularly up to the early 19th century, to supply and to crew ships to be based elsewhere and being in a region of relatively prosperous estates could finance and insure their builds. However the whole region was economically dominated by

Pwllheli and while Porthmadog's shipbuilding was more spectacular, 90% of its slate builds being squeezed into a little more than 50 years, Pwllheli built almost 30% more slate vessels and even after the establishment of the Porthmadog yards, it was Pwllheli-built ships that dealt with much of the Blaenau Ffestiniog output.

There was some metal mining and on the north coast, granite quarrying but no way could Llŷn be considered a slate producing area. There were tiny slate workings near Cricieth but only Mynydd Ednyfed SH507394 could be called a commercial enterprise and may possibly have put product aboard ship at Cricieth. There were a few diggings further east but those that preceded the founding of Porthmadog such as Bron y Foel SH554390 would have panniered product to Ynys y Cyngar SH554365 to be loaded over the beach between tides. There is little reason to suppose that Pwllheli itself handled slate although as Lewis Lloyd records that *New Expedition* left Pwllheli for Southampton on Christmas Eve 1836 with a cargo of slates from an unidentified source (possibly Mynydd Ednyfed).

The nearest the peninsular came to being directly involved in the shipment of slate was a late 19th century proposal to run rails from Hendre Ddu quarry SH519444 on the western side of Cwm Pennant to Cricieth. The sole transport development that actually took place had no slate connection. It was a road called Y Lôn Goed made by Sir Thomas Mostyn in the early 1820s to service his Plas Helen estate. Starting at Afon-wen, it was intended to reach the Caernarfon – Porthmadog road at Pantglas but only the first 4½ miles were completed, it coming to an abrupt halt at Mynydd Cennin. Tree lined, it was built virtually to 'Motorway standard' copying the Macadam graded-stone construction recently used by Telford on his Holyhead Road. (Parts with a Macadam surface, cambered and kerbed survive). There is a legend that the refusal of an elderly cottager to vacate his holding thwarted the plan, but in view of the elaborateness of construction it is more likely that the cash ran out.

Pwllheli is an ancient town long regarded as the capital of Llŷn. The elephant on the town's seal is said to derive from 'Elephant and Castle' a corruption of 'Infanta de Castille' with Plantagenet associations that allegedly derive from the 'Black Prince' who granted the town's market charter. True or false it was an important market centre, living by fishing and the shipping of and trading in, animals and agricultural products.

Like similar estuaries and creeks Pwllheli has been a harbour ever since boats were first invented and certainly by the 16th century it was an established port. The unique plumber's 'S' bend on the estuary of Afon Erch provided ample, well sheltered strands ideal to build ships, and build ships they did in numbers far in excess of local needs. Shipbuilding was in full swing by the mid-18th century and although some sloops were built, while others were concentrating on these 'Rowing-boats with masts', Pwllheli was turning out 'Proper vessels', such as brigs and brigantines of up to three figure tonnages, many to carry slate.

Before the rise of Porthmadog and the other directly slate-related harbours, Pwllheli was undisputedly the main shipbuilding centre for north Wales. Long before Porthmadog had been invented and a fleet of tiny sloops swept down the Dwyryd on the ebb of the springs, the ships into which they would perilously transfer their cargoes in the lee of Ynys Cyngar were as likely as not to be Pwllheli built, Pwllheli owned and Pwllheli manned.

By the end of the 18th century Pwllheli must have achieved some renown since in 1801 *Mary* a full square-rigged 3-masted ship that at 429 tons was a 'super tanker' of its day, was completed for Liverpool owners. By 1824 when *Two*

*Brothers* became the first Porthmadog ship, Pwllheli had launched over 250.

By this time dynasties of shipbuilders were starting to emerge, the Griffiths', Thomas', Richards', Henrys and Humphreys; as well as families such as Richard and Robert Lewis, John and Richard Pritchard, Emanuel, Lewis and Robert Evans, John, Owen and William Jones, John and David Williams, as well as the likes of Robert Davies, John Ellis, Hugh Thomas, Owen Roberts, Griffith Jones, Owen Owens and Hugh Morris, although several of these individuals only produced one vessel. There was a surge of building in the late 1840s when vessels in the 400-ton bracket were almost the norm with the Barque *William Carey* being a 659-tonner.

It is said that at one time there were 28 ships in various stages of construction at Pwllheli, which when one realises the requirements for ropes, blocks, sails and fittings of every kind, not to speak of hundreds of tons of timber, gives an indication of the scale of the industry. The size of vessels tended to fall during the 1850s; even so the 693-ton *Margaret Pugh* was launched in 1862.

David Williams having built 10 vessels in a dozen years launched the 169-ton brigantine *Carl & Louise* in 1878, the very last of almost 440 ships to be built in Pwllheli since records began in 1779. Of course it is sobering to realise that many of the larger vessels were for 'Liverpool Owners' which often meant they were for the Slave Trade, in fact the *Margaret Pugh* was openly described as being 'suitable for 600 slaves'. With emancipation beginning in America only a year after its completion, it must have been one of the last of the 'slavers'.

Of the almost 300 Pwllheli-built ships for which complete records still exist, only 31 survived to be broken up, hence presumably nearly 90% of the builds were lost, almost all in unknown locations and probably in most cases with all on board. Since there is no reason to suppose that Pwllheli vessels were more prone to loss that others – the reverse was undoubtedly true – one realises the scale of the tribute demanded by the sea for mariners as a whole.

The fame of Pwllheli vessels spread far beyond the British Isles. One schooner, *Confidence* built by Richard Pritchard in 1845 despite being a mere 87 tons, put itself, its captain and its place of origin on the map by assisting Garibaldi during the Italian war of independence of the 1860s, sadly it did not long survive, being lost off Milford Haven in 1869. In 1895 another of Richard Pritchard's builds, the rather larger (150-ton, 3-masted) schooner *Theda* sailed from Labrador to Gibraltar in less than 12 days, a record still unbeaten by a working sailing vessel. Again this fine ship sank off Fleetwood the following year.

The most prolific shipbuilding firm was William Jones & Son. William and his son David launched almost 30 ships between 1827 and 1858, but William in addition to building ships was a ship owner and ran a timber yard that made him the largest merchant in the town. He and his main competitor David Evans brought in shipload after shipload of great baulks of softwood for ship's cladding. Most came from Canada after the traditional Baltic sources dried up during the Napoleonic wars. Some hardwood for framing came from local fellings, (with the bark for the tanners a useful by-product) the rest they would buy in from along the coast.

Unlike most shipbuilders who were practical shipwrights, William started out as a druggist and would have had to employ men with carpentry experience. The term carpenter nowadays implies lesser skills than say joiner or cabinetmaker but used to be far from being the case. Admittedly *y gof* (the blacksmith) was held in some awe due to the infernal connotations of his forge but it was *y saer* (the carpenter) who was regarded as the aristocrat among tradesmen. Even an architect no matter how eminent would be accorded no better title than *y pensaer* (lit. The head carpenter).

The marine carpenter would typically have gained experience in the heavy and exacting work of constructing the timber-framed houses of the posher type of person. He would consider himself far superior to y *saer maen* (the 'stone carpenter'), who in his eyes just piled one stone upon another and called it a cowhouse or a cottage.

A shipwright/carpenter needed to be capable of selecting standing oaks for ribs and keelsons and if need be fell them. Then saw and adze them into beams and components on an heroic scale often to plans that he himself had drawn up, then bore and chisel joints and carve embellishments to hairbreadth accuracy. He would be able to steam the thickest plank into the most intricate shape and woe betide the merchant who sold him any timber that proved to be less than perfect.

The using of only the best materials in the best possible way, the spacing of ribs an inch or two less than even the soberest caution demanded, the attention to detail that charaterised every one of the builders all along the coast was legendary. It arose partly of course from an innate pride but also because owners who staked their fortunes and the seamen who staked their lives on the soundness of the vessel were likely to be friends, relatives, neighbours or members of the same chapel.

In 1841 Pwllheli is shown as having 5 shipbuilders finding work for 39 shipwright/carpenters plus 9 sawyers (lesser skilled woodworkers) and providing custom for 7 painters, 7 blacksmiths, 3 rope makers and a block maker.

It must not be forgotten that building was only part of a shipyard's work, vessels would need frequent repair, and Pwllheli with its ample space would have attended to many a Welsh vessel that had limped home under jury rig having endured perhaps weeks of fiendish pounding in some distant ocean.

It is heartening to think that the skills that might have been lost when iron displaced wood have in a measure been preserved in the working of slate. Despite not having slate of its own Pwllheli has been able to act as an overflow for Porthmadog as a slate-manufacturing centre, the respected firm of John Williams being located there. Happily its tradition is carried on by Messrs Cerrig Ltd, although sadly much of their skills are now exercised on non-slate materials.

Besides building, manning and repairing ships, the Pwllheli district was a source of finance for the north Wales maritime trade generally. In addition the Pwllheli and Nevin Mutual Marine Insurance Association of 1843, although initially unsuccessful, came to dominate marine insurance in northern Wales and continued to do so well into the steamship era. The seafaring tradition was carried on by the men of Pwllheli long after the last local ship had cleared its bar, by crewing and captaining a large slice of the British Merchant fleet.

The price of such participation has been heavy: Invariably whenever from *Birkenhead* to *Titanic*, 'Women and Children First!' has been the cry, in some port, or harbour or tiny creek in Wales a widow has been made.

# Mawddach

Like Pwllheli, afon Mawddach in general and Barmouth in particular, supplied ships and crews to Porthmadog. Unlike Pwllheli it did have some commercially viable occurrences of slate in its hinterland, but although central Meirionnydd is solid Cambrian slate-bearing rock, save for a few places where geological quirks offer tempting tasters, its slate lies deep beyond the reach of man. Small though the quantities were they still had to be transported, but the three-dozen slate producers that have been identified in the area were widely spread and so had to make their own individual transport arrangements. This was a particular challenge since roads usable by wheeled vehicles were few, and except where needed by big estates, were ill maintained. To reach Harlech, the county seat until 1870, from Dolgellau overland involved an incredible journey over the Rhinogs where stagecoach passengers often had to manhandle the vehicle up stony gradients.

The little Gwanas slate quarry SH798160 perilously perched like a hilltop diadem at almost 2000', built an 'Alpine' roadway that snaked down to the main road near Cross Foxes. Cefn Gam SH680246 high in the Rhinogian fastnesses built a road to join with a pre-existing track up Cwm Mynach, both probably expending more effort on their roads than their quarries. Product from Penrhyngwyn SH704149 on the northern flanks of Cadair Idris made its way to the Mawddach at Penmaenpool, while smaller workings around Dolgellau probably did so to Llanelltyd. In most case pack animals would have played a bigger role than carts. At tiny Moel y Gwartheg SH681320 material was probably carried away at the end of each day on the backs of the diggers themselves.

Just two quarries were able to reach navigable water by rail, Arthog SH650151 that had an incline to a jetty on the Mawddach and Tyddyn Sieffre SH630135 that had a horse tramway to a little quay at Fegla Fawr.

The commercial centre of the area was Dolgellau near the traditional lowest bridge point of the Mawddach. It is not on the river itself but is on the Wnion, which was canalised from the town to its confluence with the Mawddach to allow the passage of shallow-draught barges. Dolgellau was overwhelmingly a wool town, spinning and weaving being cottage industries, with just the initial fulling being done in mills. Unlike say, the English Cotswolds the wool trade was not lucrative since it was in the grip of the Shrewsbury Drapers who through a monopoly granted by Edward IV in 1462, had a right to buy every piece of cloth produced at prices they set.

The only other centre of population was Barmouth; in some ways a place without a past since it scarcely existed until Tudor times when it was described as having four houses. The occupants of these were probably engaged in ferrying and herring fishing with the first record of a 'Foreign' ship anchoring there being *Maru* of Fishguard in 1566, with *Le Angell de Bermo* being in 1587, the first ship known to have been based there. Such ships would have been bringing in supplies that could not be produced locally and would tend to take out timber for Pwllheli and tanbark for Ireland.

As a port Barmouth experienced a fillip in the mid 18th century when the Shrewsbury Draper's monopoly on woollen goods was found to be unenforceable so what had been a small and covert contraband activity became a substantial trade. Unfortunately this trade proved short lived since the American War of Independence closed the main markets (and caused several vessels to be captured), then the French Wars did likewise and by the time trading was resumed the modernised Yorkshire woollen industry could undercut the Welsh producers. Actually this interruption co-incided with the expansion of the slate trade, Blaenau slate providing alternative cargoes for Barmouth vessels and led to their great participation in the carriage of slate.

As regards shipping, few coasts pose a greater danger to sailing ships than the northern reaches of Bae Ceredigion between the Dwyryd and the Mawddach, they are almost perpetually on the lee with a swell that fetches from Venezuela. Open beaches, marshes and sand dunes in the north discouraged landings, loadings and certainly shipbuilding. In addition the mysterious St Patrick's Causeway that runs out arrow-straight forming a mythical road to Ireland could and still can trap even the wariest coastal seafarer.

Inshore sailing is in respects more perilous that deep-sea sailing. Whilst it is said that the coastal sailor fears being out of sight of land, the deep-sea sailor's fear of seeing land is better founded. In the wide ocean a tight, well-crewed ship can ride almost any peril, but the coaster is in constant danger of rocks and lee shores, doubly so in an engineless sailing vessel. In darkness the deep-sea man can await the dawn, by dawn the coastal man may have been wrecked and drowned.

There was just one river on this stretch of coast, the Artro. The river Artro is geographically inconsequential serving merely as a traditional division between the administrative districts of Ardudwy is-Artro and Ardudwy uwch-Artro. However industrially it was most important, its waters used and re-used powered half a dozen industries at Llanbedr making it a manufacturing centre for Harlech and a wide swathe of hinterland. The notable 18th century tombstones at Llandanwg church having almost certainly originated at Cae'n y Coed, would have been shipped at Maentwrog and landed at the Pensarn wharf using the ship's own rigging as a crane. Several ships were built at Pensarn, some to assuage the Dwyryd's insatiable demand for vessels and when in the mid-19th century Llanfair slate quarry SH580288 was first opened, its slate was loaded here for perilous coast-hugging journeys. It is also possible that manganese was shipped from here.

The Mawddach itself, whose estuary separates the sands of Dyffryn from the rocky cliffs of Friog, provided a number of creeks where ships could be berthed and indeed built safe from surf and storms. The area had an advantage over Pwllheli for shipbuilding, in the abundance of its indigenous hardwood timber, both alongside the estuary and on the extensive Nannau estate. It was asserted (Usually by persons having a vested interest in the matter) that Vale of Maentwrog timber was superior to the Mawddach article. There may be some vestige of truth in this since much of the former grew on north-facing slopes from whence timber generally proves to be tougher and more durable.

From the later 18th century when wool and slate drove ship construction, until c1880 when Canadian competition and the demand for steel hulls conspired with the impact of the railway to end shipbuilding; around 350 ships were built on the Mawddach. It is not possible to tell exactly which were built in each creek as so many, particularly in the early days, were just described as 'Barmouth built'. Some would have been built at Barmouth itself, others at creeks upstream and others launched upstream and towed to Barmouth for fitting out.

Lewis Lloyd's list commences in 1744 with the sloop *Industry* but it is 197 ships later in 1802 that anything other than 'Barmouth' or 'Wales' or even 'Britain' appears; when *Union* a snow of 106 tons is shown as having been built at Llanelltyd bridge and *Endeavour* at Rhyddallt. The next completion shown is a year later at Maesygarnedd (A little downstream of Llanelltyd bridge, where a bend in the river brings deep water to the north bank) of *Belinda* a brig of 139 tons and in fact a further two vessels came off the stocks there that year. Storehouse (a wharf and warehouse on the southern bank a little below Llanelltyd bridge) appears in 1803 with a sloop of 62 tons, *Elizabeth*.

In the first 35 years or so Barmouth builds had overwhelmingly been sloops with no vessel other than a few brigs of around 100 tons, being over 80 tons, a brig of 140 tons being a surprising 1750 exception. In 1779 there were 2 brigs of 120 and 150 tons respectively, probably built by William Jones who was a 'big ship' man. Although small sloops continued to predominate, brigs and other more substantial vessels start to come off the Barmouth stocks to meet the longer-voyage requirements not only of the Dwyryd, but also of Porth Penrhyn, Porth Dinorwig and Caernarfon.

Once into the 19th century, sloops become the minority and during the first 25 years 16 vessels are identified as Barmouth built, 17 as Maesgarnedd, 7 as Llanelltyd, with Storehouse 3, Penmaenpool 2, Rhydallt & Aberamffra 1 each, with 26 not precisely identified. It is probable that in the previous century there was a similar spread of build locations. The cramped nature of Barmouth is illustrated by an account of the launching of the schooner *Hirnant* which overhung the main street to such an extent that the traditional bottle-breaking was conducted from a bedroom window on the landward side of the street!

After 1825 when the yards at Porthmadog/Borth y Gest 'came on stream', the rate of builds tapered off, there being 2 sloops built at Storehouse in 1826 and 1834 respectively and a 41 ton schooner and a 106 ton brig at Llanelltyd in 1826 and 1827. 16 ships of up to about 100 tons were built at Griffith Davies' yard at Maesgarnedd, the last being the 80-ton schooner *Glyn* in 1865. At Barmouth 23 were built, most by John Jones, whose yard was taken over by his son Rees Jones after he retired in the early 1840s. Rees built some half a dozen until in 1849 when with the business outlook at Barmouth poor, he relocated to Porth Dinorwig. After his departure only 2 more vessels were ever built at Barmouth, one in 1854 and the last in 1857.

Penmaenpool apparently not having had a launch since 1806 was reactivated by Ellis Evans when he built the 69-ton schooner *Cambrian Maid* in 1841. It is interesting to speculate on the excitement that there must have been when the rumour first got around that Ellis was going to lay a keel. There would be speculation as to the identity of the customer and discussion as to who would be master. Opinions on rigs and pronouncements on hull design would dominate barroom chat. Elderly carpenters would have looked out their shipwrighting tools, blacksmiths and block makers would canvass for orders. Timber merchants such as Watcyn Anwyl and other tradesmen would discreetly tout. Ellis, if he was a drinking man would have been unlikely to have been allowed to stand a round, and if he owed any favours he would doubtless have been circumspectly reminded of them.

Ellis and his successors Edward Jones and David Jones built a further 12 vessels ranging from a 26-ton sloop to a 227-ton barque, up to the Mawddach's last ever build the 39-ton dory *John*, launched by David Jones in 1865. Curiously although square rig had virtually disappeared from the Mawddach stocks since the late 1820s, several of the last builds at Maesygarnedd were either brigs or brigantines. The singletons at Aberamffra (About a mile upstream from Barmouth) and Rhyddlallt (Just upstream from the village of Bont Ddu) do not seem to have been repeated, but 8 ships are from unidentified sites in that period so the record is incomplete.

In the 1869 the Cambrian Railways coastal line and the Great Western Ruabon to Dolgellau line came face to face in a buffer-to-buffer standoff at Dolgellau. Despite sharing a mutual triumph that the London and North Western had been thwarted, the two companies, each had its own separate facilities at Dolgellau right down to two turntables, all divided in an apartheid-like manner by what the financial world would come to term 'Chinese walls' that no employee of either company would dare cross.

The coming of the railways significantly benefited such quarries as Henddôl SH619122 and Golwern SH621122 to develop and attract investment and a proper settlement pattern, although their planned tramway to the railway at Fairbourne was never laid. Tyddyn Shiefre turned their tramway so that loadings could be made onto rail at Barmouth Junction rather than at the wharf at Fegla Fawr. The railway enabled Egryn quarry SH605205 to promote itself from an inconsequential scratching to a bona-fide business and it helped the several small diggings at Harlech to load onto rail via the little Harlech Tramway.

Penrhyngwyn and Cefn Gam could load onto rail at Penmaenpool rather than use the river. Llanfair could load onto the Cambrian, instead of using the sketchy facilities at Pensarn harbour and enabled it to enter into an agreement with Penarth quarry near Corwen to process some of their material, co-operation that had hitherto been impossible. Similarly it became possible for Inigo Jones at Caernarfon to source 'Enamelling friendly' material from Cae Defaid SH720160 and Cwmerau SH777107.

The line's arrival encouraged Arthog to abandon its jetty and to invest heavily in a new mill with a grand incline to a trans-shipment siding rail, a step that unfortunately proved to be a financially fatal.

The railways brought a further bonus to the small slate quarries. Although remote units such as Cae Defaid still had to cart a fair distance, the railways' ability to accept small quantities for immediate dispatch enabled them to react more quickly to customers' requirements than had they still been tied to water. Thus the small marginal units were helped to take advantage of the 1860s/1870s slate boom. Furthermore, in areas like Mawddach the quarries were too small and dispersed to support local suppliers such as foundries and stockists of oils, tools, ropes, chains and so on. The railways and their concomitant telegraph facility enabled spares and consumables to be obtained in hours, obviating the need for large 'just in case' inventories.

Although shipbuilding and seafaring brought about the development of Barmouth, Llanelltyd and riverside communities, slate quarrying and its transport were mostly too disparate to influence settlement patterns, Arthog with half a dozen slate workings within walking distance, giving rise to quarry-built dwellings including a nice terrace, being an exception. Arthog could later claim some fame in the wider world when Arthog Hall a mock-gothic castle built by a cotton-mill owner from Lancashire was adopted as name for GWR Hall class locomotive 6993.

Nearby Fairbourne had no slate significance being a seaside settlement created out of a ferry hamlet, a conversion enabled by the railway, the very agency whose viaduct had made its previous role redundant.

It had been predicted that the railway would finish shipping – in fact when the Barmouth viaduct was proposed the railway company arrogantly attempted to dismiss the requirement that it should be openable on the grounds that no more ships would use the Mawddach! The railway did of course boost tourism and had some influence on shipping, but supplies continued to be delivered to Barmouth by regular coasting steamships until almost the mid 20th century.

Dolgellau's slate associations are too dilute to have had much influence upon it, its importance as a market town being augmented in the 1860s by the railways and in the 1870s by it wresting county-town status from Harlech. Plus, of course its 'Gold Rush' in the last decades of the 19th century when it became the focal point of the Dolgellau Gold Belt. Few of the dozens of gold diggings ever actually produced metal and less than a handful made a profit over more than a year or two, even so enough optimism persisted to justify ironmongers stocking gold-panning pans for a further century.

# 7

# DYFI

Afon Dyfi appears to resemble afon Mawddach in that both
are rivers running northeast – southwest, each having a port
at the north of its estuary (Aberdyfi and Barmouth) and each
with a town of some importance near its lowest bridge-point
(Machynlleth and Dolgellau), each with an adjacent river-port
(Derwen-las and Llanelltyd) as well as creeks and shipping
points on their lower reaches. Both built ships in some
numbers, but whereas Mawddach's dominant activity was not
slate, on the Dyfi it definitely was.

Some slate was won on each side of the Dyfi estuary and
some in its valley proper with other occurrences in the narrow
defile of its tributary river Angell, but the most abundant slate
was found in the Dulas valley, centred on Corris. The earliest
known commercial working at neighbouring Aberllefenni
began at least in the 15th century, this early development
being made possible by quarrying right alongside an ancient
road enabling output to be carried down the eastern side of
the Dulas valley to the river Dyfi at Derwen-las. Although
called a 'road' its gradients and in winter its mud, even after
successive improvements, made a cart journey a laborious
affair with stones and pot holes that were liable to reduce a
load of best slates to worthless shards.

Slate had been won at Upper Corris from at least the 18th
century but it was only when Sir John Edwards the local
landowner built the present road down the western side of the
Dulas Valley in the 1830s that serious working there became

possible. However it soon became apparent that the cost of cartage even on this improved road, made their slate uncompetitive with the same Ordovician material coming down from Blaenau Ffestiniog via the new Ffestiniog Railway. From the 1840s there were a number of proposals for building a similar railway to serve the Corris area slate workings. The obvious destination for such a line would be Derwen-las but it was already well occupied by Aberllefenni quarry and the facilities at Cei Ward a little further downstream were dominated by various lead mining companies. In any case both quays were limited to vessels of around 70 tons. So whilst a branch on the south side of the river was not ruled out, it was felt that any rail line should seek more space and deeper water on the north bank of the Dyfi at Ynys, Fron Goch or even Aberdyfi, any of which would give the added bonus that slate could be picked up from several quarries on the way.

Eventually in 1859 largely through the efforts of Arthur Coulston anxious to develop his Braich Goch quarry SH748078, the Corris, Machynlleth and River Dyfi Tramroad came into being. Starting at Aberllefenni village it ran through Derwen-las to Cei Ward. Formations were built but never railed, for a short extension to Llwyn Bwtri where there was some shipbuilding and a ferry to Pennal, but being on the inside of a bend on the river it would scarcely have been an ideal place for a wharf. The proposal to find deeper and less tidal-dependent water at Garreg (Glandyfi) was never put into effect.

A branch, the Upper Corris Tramway, served the quarries there; another the Ratgoed Tramway served Ratgoed SH787119 and Cwmerau SH777107 quarries and a third, the Aberllefenni Branch the actual Aberllefenni quarries SH768103. Short spurs served the Eescairgeiliog Mill SH769059 and Llyngwern SH757045 quarry. In the next few years there were ideas of extending the Upper Corris branch to Cross Foxes to pick up ironstone, but this was abandoned when the lack of potential was realised. The formations were actually built for a branch to serve the Glyn Iago SH719072 and Tynyberth SH738087 slate quarries, but again this was sensibly abandoned for similar reasons.

Sadly the good slatemen of Corris found themselves in a no-win situation, this fine horse drawn railway that would put their transport costs on a par with Blaenau was almost immediately outdated by the steaming of the Ffestiniog Railway in 1863.

Then followed further problems – the standard gauge main line arrived from Newtown and pressed on past Machynlleth to parallel the Corris line at Derwen-las. Not only did this thundering juggernaut frighten the horses but also in due time rendered the quays almost unusable due to the railway formations diverting the river. Eventually the lower section of the Tramroad had to be abandoned and all slate loaded onto the main line at Machynlleth station.

The Newtown – Machynlleth main line's arrival enabled the Mawddwy Railway to be built. Although a private line it functioned as a branch to carry material from the Minllyn quarry SH852139 at Dinas Mawddwy to the main line at Cemmaes Road. The Mawddwy Railway also handled material brought to its Aberangell station by the Hendre Ddu Tramway from the Hendre Ddu quarry SH799125. This quaint little 2' gauge (or so!) tramway was also connected to three other workings in the slate-rich Angell valley and acted as a real 'social' transport link along this roadless valley for in addition to its branches to the slate quarries, spurs provided a door-to-door service to several farms. Originally horse-drawn – the leisurely progress of neither its freight nor its workmen's trains disturbed the solitude of this sylvan valley. Later when forestry haulage predominated, Petrol and Diesel 'lash-ups' were used.

The Hendre Ddu tramway was something of a curiosity, but even more singular was the Cae Baty line a mere half mile in length it brought material to Minllyn quarry from the small Cae Baty SH846136 working in the next valley. It comprised a short level section on a little plateau with an incline downward at each end. A stationary engine sited at the middle of the level section could haul trucks up one incline, with down going trucks on the other incline forming a partial counterbalance by means of a lengthy rope between them.

Slate was found at several sites on the northern bank of the estuary, two with their own little railways. One, Frongoch SH664872 occupied a compact site that worked a pit accessed by a tunnel, it had a steam mill as well as dwellings huddled together near the water's edge. Although the main line railway crossed over the site it distained connection and continued to load onto boats until a storm wrecked its own little pier. Of more consequence was Cwm Ebol SH689017 at Pennal. It had become clear that a tramway along the north bank was never going to happen and that the Machynlleth-Aberdyfi railway was going to remain on the south bank until further downstream. Therefore seeing no chance of rail connection, in 1865 Cwm Ebol quarry built a tramway to the river at the site of the Roman ford at Llyn Bwtri. This 1½-mile, 3' (later 2') gauge line, was notable in that it was the very last railed route laid down to convey slates to water, thereafter every subsequent slate quarry line would be to a main line railway.

The Dyfi and its tributary valleys were not the only sources of slate, there being a score of workings in the Dysenni valley to the north. There was a shipping point on the Dysenni's little estuary at Tywyn, but from the 18th century it was too convoluted and too silted to permit the passage of much more than a rowing boat. The sole significant producer, Bryneglwys SH695054 pack horsed over the mountains to Pennal via Cwm Ebol to load onto the river at Llyn Bwtri. When

Bryneglwys was taken over and developed in 1864 the new owners laid down the Tal-y-llyn Railway, a 2' 3" gauge line that had a double significance. When the River Dyfi Tramroad had been built there had been no question of it being steam powered, scarcely half a dozen years later, following the success of the steaming of the Ffestiniog Railway there was no question of the Tal-y-llyn not being steamed. Thus it was the very first new-build narrow gauge steam railway to serve a slate quarry. Probably of more significance was the fact that it was the first dedicated slate quarry railway built to terminate at a main line exchange rather than at a shipping place. (Although naming its lower terminus Wharf Station did confer some maritime flavour!)

Another notable feature of the Tal-y-llyn was that although it was built and owned by the one quarry company it was a public line running passenger services to a timetable, (As it still does 1½ centuries later). In addition it very directly served the community. Emulating Samuel Holland who had built houses alongside the Ffestiniog Railway to give them direct rail access, the Tal-y-llyn had a branch specifically to serve on a door-to-door basis the two rows of houses that the quarry had built between two pre-existing hamlets to create the village of Abergynolwyn. The intention was not only to deliver coal and other household supplies, but also to take away the contents of the earth privies for sale to farmers. (This would seem to give a whole new dimension to making a profit out of the workforce!). This branch on the valley floor, reached from the railway by a self-acting incline, besides delivering suppliers to the houses and shops, (and beer to the pub) it served a small writing-slate factory intended to be staffed by women and by men too old to face the stiff climb to the quarry itself.

This Tal-y-llyn line made the clanking concocotion that was the River Dyfi Tramway look sick indeed, and it was with resounding cheers that it was steamed in 1879, retaining the same 2' 3" gauge. Unfortunately it failed to bring cheer to the quarry owners who were in the depths of a recession. On top of this it was too lightly trafficked for its rates to put them on level terms with the Ffestiniog producers. What is more the quarries it served failed to match the 1890s recovery in trade that the Ffestiniog people enjoyed. Although it survived post-WW2 it in fact became almost an anachronism when the Braich Goch Quarry Co failed in 1906.

However since it was a full passenger-carrying railway, it was able to contribute to education, it and lines like it enabled children from outlying settlements to attend secondary schools as day-pupils. It is doubtful if the distinguished surgeon, Alfred William Hughes F.R.C.S., son of Robert Hughes; manager of Aberllefenni quarry could ever have become a medical man without being able to attend school in Machynlleth by courtesy of the Corris Railway.

Abergynolwyn, Corris, Upper Corris, Aberllefenni and Ceinws were slate-generated settlements as were Aberangell and Dinas Mawddwy. However the commercial epicentre of the area was Machynlleth that represented the tip of the Norman Marcher Lordships' finger that thrust between Ceredigion and Meirionnydd creating a 'Window on the world' for Montgomeryshire (and incidentally splitting north Wales from the south). It was primarily a market town, and although livestock no longer cavort in Maengwyn Street, the market licensed by Edward I in 1291 has been held there each Wednesday ever since. The foundry that served the quarries is sadly no longer there but slate is still traded in the town much as it has been for more than half a millennium.

The port of Machynlleth was of course Derwen-las

comprising Cei Ellis and Cei Tafarn Isa, with Cei Ward a little further downstream and beyond it Llyn Bwtri, all collectively classed as Morben. Although an ancient lead ore exporting point, by the early 1860s with the tramroad newly arrived, its 100 tons of ore was exceeded 15-1 by slate, the latter even exceeding the timber exports. Long before the tramroad, long before these wharves existed, there was activity here. Presumably the Romans supplied their fort at Cefn Caer via the river and writings from the 12th century infer shipping hereabouts. Lead and slate were being loaded here by the 16th century at least and by the 18th century trade was in full swing and the village of Derwen-las could be regarded as a genuine port. Tanbark, timber, wool and farm-produce were shipped from much of Montgomeryshire as well as from southern Meirionnydd and northern Ceredigion, giving it an importance beyond its size. Grain was landed, as was limestone to feed the village's limekilns as well as culm to fire them and to mix with clay to provide cottage fuel for those unable to cut peat. Coal and wine, the two great indulgences of the rich as well as tea, the indulgence of the super-rich and all sorts of shop goods (£14,000 p.a. mid 19th century) were brought in for the comparatively affluent town of Machynlleth. That the citizens were 'Well-heeled' is shown by the hundreds of hides brought in for its many shoemakers.

Although the pools on the river enabled small sea-going vessels to reach Derwen-las, a great deal of the river traffic was transferred into larger ships at Aberdyfi, a place that, in contrast to Barmouth, is mentioned in 12th century writings. Certainly active in Elizabethan times, there being record of a Spanish ship taking refuge in the river in 1587, but anchored out of musket range and the military being unable to borrow a boat this (enemy) vessel was immune from attack. Equally risibly in 1599 a French ship arrived salt-laden just when on the opposite shore of the estuary, attempts were being made to make salt by trapping and evaporating the ebb-tides, unaware that the war-created salt shortage was over.

By this time Aberdyfi had its own herring fishing fleet and of course, the ferry had been very long established. At one time there were three ferryboats one to carry foot passengers, another to carry horsemen and carts, with a third to carry carriages, with suitably graded fares. It remained a perilous crossing with currents that defeated at least two attempts to build a Barmouth style viaduct. By the 18th century Aberdyfi was busy as a trans-shipment point for cargoes coming down river, not that that activity was universally welcomed. When boats tied up en-route due to darkness or an ebbing tide, the crews would make camp on the bank, much to the annoyance of riverside landowners.

It is perhaps not so much for trade as for shipping and shipbuilding that the Dyfi area is known. These were very much communal activities often financed by persons of very modest means indeed, farmers, shopkeepers and certainly mariners, even the proverbial 'Widows and Orphans' had their one or two sixty-fourths.

The first ship recorded as being built at Aberdyfi itself was the 26-ton sloop *Linnet* in 1769, but this would certainly not have been the first and in any case would have been antedated by up-river builds. In the latter part of the 18th century more than 20 vessels were completed on the Dyfi some at Garreg, at least one at Llugwy, but although the name Derwen-las does not appear until 1802, several ships had already been built there, in fact in 1761 *Nelly* a 27-ton sloop was probably built at Derwen-las. Most of the river-builds were sloops and although a few were over 60 tons most would have been less than half that size. It is interesting that the rate of build in the 1770s/80s was almost a ship a year but there was only one completion recorded between 1789 and 1802, a doldrums situation that contrasted with the Mawddach's brisk activities at that time.

During the first two decades of the 19th century almost 30 ships were built in the area, 4 at Aberdyfi (none after 1804), 6 up the coast at Tywyn (including a snow of 123 tons), 2 at Garreg and the rest at Derwen-las/Morben, whose builds started to include square-rigs of up to 150-tons. After a 20-year lull between 1817 and 1837, when only 4 were built (all at Derwen-las), things started up again with the sloop *Patriot* being launched at Aberdyfi in 1838. From then until 1860 almost 40 vessels averaging around 50 tons with one as small as 13 tons and just a couple exceeding 100 tons were built, the sloops of earlier years being largely replaced by schooners. Approximately two thirds were built at Aberdyfi; where in 1858 Roger Lewis launched *Aberllefenni Quarry Maid* a 58-ton schooner which was immediately sailed to Caernarfon to have its 50-hp steam engine installed by Messrs De Winton. This vessel, not to be confused with the 89-ton schooner *Quarry Maid* launched by Jones & Co at Pwllheli four years earlier for the Porthmadog trade, was commissioned by Col. R. D. Pryce of Aberllefenni to take advantage of the then new tramroad that was about to serve his quarry. This was a very early use of steam for a north Wales sea-going vessel, although a De Winton-engined tug built at Bangor had been supplied to Barmouth in 1856 and Aberdyfi had a Liverpool-built steam tug in 1861.

Roger Lewis was a master mariner untrained in construction, nevertheless he built a number of vessels between 1848 and 1879, and at least one, *Napoleon* a 54-ton schooner he commanded himself.

Nothing more was heard of shipbuilding at either Tywyn or Garreg but John Evans built 3 ships at Morben between 1864 and 1867, two being brigs of 99 tons and 200 tons respectively, the third a barque *Mary Evans* launched in 1867 was despite the restricted depth of water a massive 254 tons. However during the 1860s and 1870s this lack of water upriver meant that most builds were at Aberdyfi itself where in the early 60s the Owens built 3 80/90-ton schooners and Roger Lewis built his last two schooners, one in 1866 and another in 1879.

The most prominent builder was John Jones, believed to have been a Porthmadog-trained ships' carpenter who built 29 vessels mainly schooners between 1849 and the early 1870s, most at his yards at Aberdyfi but two at Llwyn Bwtri and one at a rather isolated site at Ynys-las on the other side of the estuary, where Henry Harries of Llansantffraid had built the 124 ton schooner *Island Maid* in 1852. Around 1860 there were 6 yards busy at Aberdyfi with Jones being responsible for 16 launches in 7 years. During the 1870s the torch for Aberdyfi shipbuilding was held by Thomas Richards who having built 5 schooners, a smack and a brig since 1848, built 7 schooners in that last decade, poignantly his final keel, that of the 99-ton schooner *Olive Branch*, he laid down but did not live to see its 1880 launch.

For the usual reasons there were no more ships ever built at Aberdyfi yards – but not from Ynys-las where these days Steel-Kit Ltd produce 'flat-pack' kit vessels in steel plate, that can be weld-assembled in the most primitive and remote locations.

Long before Richards' *Olive Branch* had taken the water, the main line railway had arrived. Most slate ports were adversely affected by the railway, but Aberdyfi most certainly was not. Admittedly the river traffic all but vanished, but slate converged on Aberdyfi from the Mawddwy Railway and its Hendre Du feeder, from the Corris line and its several branches, from the Tal-y-llyn Railway (delivered in quarry wagons on transporter trucks), and indeed a modicum from Aberdyfi itself, the Alltgoch quarry SH620964 having been resuscitated. Whilst a great deal of this slate stayed on the railway to be delivered to other ports and to inland destinations, a great deal did not - leading to the rapid development of the Aberdyfi harbour facilities with a pier and wharves served by a railway spur coming in from the north. The railway also enabled Aberdyfi harbour to develop new business, such as the landing of cattle from Ireland for onward carriage by rail to the big English city abattoirs.

Aberdyfi also handled imports and exports for Tywyn including supplies in and out of Tywyn's big flourmill, unfortunately this mill duplicated a similar mill at Aberdyfi, so that it had to re-invent itself as a slate factory.

The railways ushered in the age of the iron hull and steam propulsion, this was the greatest of news for sailors – there was heat to dry clothes and bedding, hot water to wash and power to steer clear of lee shores and perhaps best of all, no going aloft in gales to shorten sail.

It is not always realised how old the steamship is, long before the steam tugs, paddle steamers were reaching north Wales from Liverpool in the 1820s and from 1834 *Vale of Clwyd* was a regular visitor and in 1863 *Elizabeth* began working as a ferry between Aberdyfi and Ynys-las. By that time the steamers of the Cambrian Steam Packet Company were offering fortnightly services between Liverpool and London, calling at all the main north Wales ports. The Aberdyfi and Barmouth Steamship Company ran services to Ireland and up to WW1 Messrs David Jones & Co weekly boat in from Liverpool was met by grocer's boys with hand-trucks. Aberdyfi continued to function up to WW2 as a steamship port although few were involved in the slate trade.

There was one respect by which railways greatly benefited the slate industry in the central Ceredigion area – slate enamelling. Initially developed at Aberllefenni, this was a mid 19th century bid to widen the market for slate slab products by making them look like something more exotic. The first examples were 'mock marble', but a variety of finishes were available and such was the craze for enamelled slate that the process applied to almost any household object that could be made out of slate and be made not to look like slate. Wood grain was popular but even a 'Slate finish' was in demand.

The slate in the Dyfi area not only lent itself to slab product manufacture, but also withstood the heat of the enamelling process, so that enamelling spread from Aberllefenni to Corris, Ceinws, Machynlleth and Tywyn, and even when it was done further afield Dyfi slate was usually specified. Locally the industry became centred on Aberystwyth and in the late 19th century despite there being major enamellers in south Wales, London and the north of England, local works supplied municipalities and potentates everywhere thus Aberystwyth could be regarded as the enamelling capital of the world. The most important works being Hosking and Miller who were at the back of the 'Barn' in Cambrian Street, Peter Jones, in Charlie's Stores' present premises in Cambrian Place and William Griffiths' Aberystwyth Slate & Marble Co that had a rail connected works on Llanbadarn Road. It was of course the railways that made it all possible picking up from small, and otherwise unviable quarries on both sides of the Dyfi estuary. Several quarries such as Glandyfi SN698961, Morben SN991715 and Afon Alice SH693024 blossomed and some, including Llwyngwern SH7570450 and Glandyfi SN698951 were taken over by enamellers to safeguard supplies.

One of the industries favourite products were mantelpieces possibly on the basis that a house only need one roof but usually required up to four mantelpieces. These varied from a basic 'Two uprights and shelf' to elaborate enamelled confections. For embellishment pictures often of nice rural scenes were added usually being transfer-applied. Aberystwyth became famous for such depictions that were often artists' originals. This arose because at that time artists took up residence in seaside towns to paint visitors' pictures – the 19th century version of 'Holiday snaps' one such painter was Alfred Worthington, who finding life precarious took up the decoration of slate and was responsible for the hand-painting of quite beautiful landscapes and such, on many slate-enamelled artifacts, all of which gave Aberystwyth a special cachet in decorative slate enamelling.

Well before becoming involved in enamelling, and even before its harbour improvements of the 1840s and rail connection in the 1860s, Aberystwyth was a commercial centre serving the lead and silver mining. It is claimed that the name of the river Ystwyth derives from the Phoenicians who allegedly took metal ores from Cwm Ystwyth hundreds of years BC. One is on firmer ground speaking of its industrial associations being 16th century and that the needs of that industry eventually caused the setting up of the Ship Bank in Bridge Street in 1762. This bank not only served the mines but also facilitated the building and owning of ships and the development of maritime trade – shipping out ore and bringing a variety of supplies including culm for the limekilns and timber for the great timber merchants and shipyards. The shipyards also benefited from the four foundries set up to supply the mines and the many blacksmiths who at one time included a woman, Mary Ellis.

Although like say Pwllheli, it had no slate of its own, the vessels built, owned and crewed at Aberystwyth became very much an integral part of the Bae Ceredigion 'slate fleet', a participation was not confined to Aberystwyth itself. Besides the more than 200 ships built there by eminent builders such as John Evans and Jones & Williams, some 60 were also built on the tiny Peris river at Llansantffraid in all shapes and sizes up to the 228 tons of the square-rigged *Majestic* and around half that number again at Aberarth and another 90 at Aberaeron, many being towed as bare hulls to be fitted out at Aberystwyth.

In this mid-19th century scramble for ships, Newquay also built many vessels and if one includes nearby Traeth Gwyn and Cei Bach its total possibly exceeded that of Aberystwyth itself. It was reported in 1848 that there were 10 builds on the blocks at the same time. Although much of this shipbuilding was to meet the insatiable demand of the north Wales slate trade, the activity at these tiny ports themselves was considerable. A tariff posted by Newquay in the mid-19th century illustrates the bizarre variety of goods handled even in the smallest of ports. The list included –

| | |
|---|---|
| For every marble tombstone or monument | 5/- (25p) |
| For every hundredweight of gunpowder | 1/- (5p) |
| For every ton of salt | 1/6 (7.5p) |
| For a pianoforte | 5/- (25p) |
| For a bath chair | 1/- (5p) |
| Per ton of culm | 2d (.8p) |
| Each hundred 'cocoanuts' | 1/- (5p) |

Building ceased in the 1880s and the steamships sailed disdainfully past these tiny ports but they were likely to be crewed, mastered and owned by men from these seemingly insignificant places.

# 8

# SOUTH-WESTERN WALES

The tonnage of slate produced in south Ceredigion, north Pembrokeshire and west Carmarthenshire during slate's mid-19th century heyday scarcely amounted to 1% of the north Wales total and a year's output could be matched by Blaenau Ffestiniog in little more than a week. Yet in the early 17th century as much slate was going to Ireland from south-western Wales as from Caernarfonshire.

The industry, mainly confined to north Pembrokeshire, allegedly furnished the slate for the Roman fort of Caerleon and according to some sources, roofed Whitland Abbey in the 12th century. Certainly by the 16th century the area was regularly sending slate to Bristol, then one of the largest and most prosperous cities in Britain.

Things started to go wrong in the 18th century when the Devon and Cornwall producers made serious inroads into the Bristol Channel market. Also later in that century when there was much prestigious building in Dublin the big north Wales producers grabbed the business. Even so there was considerable expansion in southwest Wales during the 19th century, but unfriendly geology and a lack of bone fide investment meant that scarcely more than half a dozen of the scores of workings in the area ever had any sort of mechanisation. Most sawing was done by hand using a handsaw unknown elsewhere in Wales, more suited to light coppicing than the making of tombstones.

Little was sold outside the Bristol Channel/Irish Sea although there was an exception in 1841 when Bellstone quarry SN079303 received a 45-ton enquiry from Belgium, despite freight to Ostend adding over £25 (Mostly for cartage to the coast) to their somewhat optimistic £48 bid, They won the order but when Bellstone was wound up nine years later the invoice was still unpaid.

These small quarries suffered an additional handicap in that it was cheaper to roof a building in large slates than in small slates, so that a higher price per ton could be obtained for larger sizes, but generally the rock in this area did not lend itself to producing slates in large sizes and often the quality was challengeable. The resultant lower profitability was exacerbated by the fact that the large northern quarries tended to have a surplus of small sizes in the lower qualities, so having secured their profit on large Bests, could sell off the small Seconds very cheaply to clear their yards. There was also possibly a self-inflicted psychological barrier to sales – a distressingly large proportion of production turned out to be small and random sized slates. In other areas they were was sold by weight as 'Ton' slates, in this area this quasi-rubbish was termed 'Locals' undoubtedly giving rise to confusion between 'Locals' and all locally sourced slate.

Furthermore, although a slate quarry's outgoings were mostly wages, hopefully paid every 4 weeks, customers expected to be granted 6 or 12 months credit. Thus considerable capital was needed to finance the Sales Ledger so obviously the more business that was done, the greater was the capital requirement. So the under-funded quarries of this area found themselves in a 'Poverty Trap', unable to expand and often fair game for predatory speculators. Thus few could finance transport links and anyway even fewer had the traffic to justify such expenditure. So unless they were right on the coast as say Porth-gain SM813325 or had a handy river as at

Cilgerran SN195431etc and Fforest SN190450, high carriage costs remained a handicap.

When the coast was reached there was a plethora of creeks and harbours where slate could be shipped, but only one real 'slate' port – Cardigan (*Aberteifi*) on the estuary of the Teifi where slate mainly arrived by boat from the Cilgerran and Fforest quarries situated on the riverbank in the Teifi Gorge. These dozen or so riverside diggings consolidated eventually into four units, could load directly into river barges. They and their respective settlements, Cilgerran and the much smaller Fforest formed the only real 'slate area' in southwest Wales and until the quarries silted up the river by tipping into it, Cilgerran was very much a port in its own right governed by a Port Reeve and elected Aldermen (offices that still survive in an honorary form). Possibly even before the slate was exploited limestone and culm with which to burn it would have been landed at Cilgerran as well as general supplies, from the later 18th century iron, tin and coal would have been taken on up river to the Penygored tinplate works and its finished products brought down to Cardigan by lighters that were partly at least man-hauled.

Cardigan was certainly used by the Normans to supply their castle but the first known slate connection was when *Marigould* took 10,000 'Tilling Stones', (Crude slates) valued at 50/- (£2.50), probably from a small scratching such as Cwmdegwell SN163454, to Ireland in 1620. This seems to have settled down to a small but regular trade until late 18th century when the Teify Gorge workings started to be properly exploited.

Cardigan became one of Wales' leading ports. Tan bark, bricks, timber, herrings and hides were exported, tiny ships going to Spain and Portugal and following the 17th century restrictions on grain imports, corn was shipped out coastwise. Although by Porthmadog standards slate tonnages were derisory they were the dominant export of Cardigan, sending mainly to western Wales, Bristol and Bristol Channel destinations. Some Cardigan slate did reach North America, but probably only fortuitously when the very low value 'Locals' were used as ballast and were able to find a buyer at the destination.

As a port it could once claim the unique distinction of having a woman pilot, Betsi James, wife of a Master Mariner who having scrambled aboard an incoming vessel off Gwbert in her voluminous Victorian skirts, had the exacting task of conning it across the Cardigan Bar and past the treacherous Poppit Sands.

Fishing boats and other small vessels must have been built here since earliest times but the first record of a build was *Mermaid* a 25-ton sloop in 1778. Shipbuilding seems to have been in full swing by 1839 when five yards were in use at Netpool and Mwldan, with a sixth across the river at St. Dogmaels (*Llandudoch*). These yards were ideally situated on a sheltered stretch of water close to the town and with ancillary industries including sawpits, foundries, blacksmiths, sail makers, rope makers and at least one block maker adjacent. Since they suffered from shallowness of water, when the demand for larger vessels grew, both building and repairing declined and as a consequence also did the fortunes of the timber merchants and the ancillary trades, by 1850 there were just 3 yards in work. Building continued on a reduced scale until 1877 when John Williams whose Mwldan premises had been for long the leading Cardigan yard, built his last ship the 29-ton ketch *Margaret Anne*. Repair work and the breaking up of ships carried on in a small way until the end of the century. The breaking up of sailing ships only became a sizeable business in the late 19th century arising out of the need to re-equip with steamers rather than sailing them until they sank. This had a slate industry dimension since many ex-maritime items such as crab-winches found second careers in quarries.

Including St. Dogmaels over 160 ships were built in the 99 years to 1877, some were square riggers and exceeded 100 tons but predominately they were sloops averaging at best 50 tons. Besides carrying local slate many Cardigan ships carried cargoes from Porthmadog and from the Caernarfon ports.

Besides the usual reasons for the demise of shipbuilding, W. J. Lewis quotes John Williams as blaming it on the decline in the quality and longevity of ships which he ascribed to the practice of bending timber in steam boxes rather than heating them over a fire and to sawing planks rather than shaping them with adzes!

As would be expected most ships registered at the port were locally owned even when not locally built. The Lloyds of Coedmore Estate who were ship owners, partly because they were slate quarrying landowners (e.g. Henllys SN113395) had four ships - *Ruby* a 21-ton sloop was built at Cardigan but *Union* a 20-ton sloop was built nearby at Llangranog in 1813, but possibly reflecting the draught restrictions at the Cardigan yards their larger vessels were both built in southern Pembrokeshire, *William Skyrme* a 65-ton schooner at Laugharne in 1810 and *Penrhyn Castle* a 44-ton sloop at Lawrenny in 1839. The name of this latter of course confirming their participation in the northern Wales slate trade. Later in the 19th century the Stephens of Llechryd who were deeply involved with slate working at Cilgerran and Fforest and with merchanting at Cardigan, ran six ships, four being locally built with one from Aberystwyth, but their flagship the big (197-ton) Brigantine *Elizabeth Stephens* was built at Ipswich. This vessel was later owned by the Griffiths' who were also prominent in Cilgerran slate and owned lighters that took their product down river to Cardigan.

There were two foundries at Cardigan, the Bailey Foundry started by ironmonger Thomas Lloyd with partners Davies and Myers, which was conveniently sited close to the Mwldan shipyards and specialised in the making of anchors, chains, and all sorts of marine fittings and tackle. When it was taken over by Williams & Thomas it diversified into agricultural and woollen machinery and even steam engines. In 1854 it absorbed the other foundry, the Bridgend Foundry that had been started by David Davies a ship owner, limekiln operator and rope maker and in the mid 1860s the old Mwldan premises were closed. The building was almost immediately snapped up by Jeremiah Stephens the owner of Plain SN201426, the largest quarry at Cilgerran who converted it into a slate sawing and planing works. The reason being that the Cilgerran quarries had no planning machines and were losing out to planed slab coming down from north Wales. This initiative of Stephens stole a march on the other slab producing quarries who eventually had to dump their unplaned slab at cut prices. When the railway came to Cilgerran in 1885 Stephens transferred the machinery to a fine purpose-built mill above his quarry near the station. The Mwldan premises became the Cardigan Engineering & Foundry who incidentally built the coal pier.

The other slate connection at Cardigan was the Cardigan Mercantile Company, founded in 1785 at Parrog as slate agents, it dealt in a wide variety of products such as timber, coal, culm and lime (which they burned in their own kilns) as well as Cilgerran slates, also owning a fleet of ships. The firm's successors are still in business and their original Cardigan premises are now the Visitor Centre.

By the beginning of the 20th century the port was in a decline accelerated by the silting due to slate quarries tipping into the Teifi, not that this worried the quarries, since in 1885 the Whitland & Cardigan Railway provided loading facilities close to the mills and finishing areas of the three main Cilgerran producers, Plain, Cefn SN204427 & Dolbadau SN197429. Since the Fforest quarries were a spent force by the time the railway opened they never had cause to use it. The Fforest quarry 'village' long outlasted the quarries and when in 1927 the carriage of the furniture of the few surviving inhabitants may well be the last cargo carried on the river.

Despite the silting steam and later motor, vessels were based at Cardigan. They played no part in the slate but coal was delivered to the gasworks by sea until 1957.

Some slate was won from the cliffs at Lochtyn SN313545 near Llangrannog north of Cardigan, presumably to be shipped over the beach at this very much maritime-dependent community. It is astonishing that not only were more than a dozen ships built at the tiny hamlet including in 1859 *Ann Catherine* a 214-ton Brig, but many local people became ship owners in a relatively substantial way. Llangrannog was the home of Sarah Rees who crewed for her father in his ketch at the age of 13, qualified as a Master Mariner before she was 21, became a school mistress, taught music, preached and was the first woman to win an Eisteddfod Chair, she later taught navigation, her ex-pupils known as 'Cranogwen Captains' (after her Bardic Title) being regarded as the cream of their profession.

Other creeks and beaches such as Aberporth, Abercastle, Cwmtudu and Abermawr (Once the intended destination for the Great Western Railway) and even miniscule Mwnt, Tresaith and Penbryn, were involved in shipbuilding and ship owning to an extent much quite disproportionate to the size of their communities.

A few miles to the south of Cardigan is Parrog, the port of Newport long engaged in fishing, maritime trading and shipbuilding, It is recorded that in 1566, 11,000 'Tilling stones' were sent from here to Bristol. Some of the slate, which was dispatched from here, would have come from the several small cliff-top quarries towards Dinas, but some would have come in a more unusual way. West of Parrog there are a number of slate occurrences in tiny bays accessible only by boat at low tide. Parrog men would row out on the ebb to work these often by driving oak wedges into cracks in the rock. When the tide rose, the wedges would swell and dislodge blocks that could be picked up at the next low tide and brought back to Parrog for splitting into slates on the quayside and loaded into sea-going vessels. Since such work would be out of view and the wet-wedge method was silent, the cliff-top landowner would be happily unaware of these activities. Thus, free of rents, royalties and other annoyances, slate obtained from these unrecorded and ephemeral enterprises must have been modestly profitable.

The concept of a port/quarry enclave was carried to an industrial level at Porth-gain SM813325, where a real harbour with stone quays was the nucleus of a self-contained slate quarrying community, its mill was water-powered but several steam engines were used for haulage. Interestingly when the slate trade declined, the place successfully diversified first into brick making and afterwards road stone that prospered well into the 20th century. A mile or so down the coast Abereiddi SM795315 was a similar quarry/port community but its beach loading was abandoned and it was linked to the slate sawing and shipping facilities of Porthgain by a horse-drawn tramway. Remarkably for such a small undertaking, material was raised by a steam-powered lift. Also shipping out of Porthgain was the nearby Trwynllwyd SM832329 a quite remarkable working extracting from the cliff onto a tide-washed beach, the blocks being hauled to the cliff top sawmill by a ropeway powered from the sawmill's steam engine. The use of the steam at these three places was of course made possible by the ease with which coal could be shipped in from the south of the county.

Fishguard (*Abergwaun*) is mainly regarded as a fishing/packet port, with some shipbuilding but from very early times was sending slate to Ireland, which by 1639 had become was a well-established trade, 40,000 slates being loaded that year a total that at the time put them on a par with any north Wales port. These slates may have come from nearby Cronllwyn quarry SM985353 which was developed during the 19th century and had it not struck the 'hards' that caused its mid 1860s closure, might have had its own railway to Fishguard.

South of St David's head is Solva (*Solfach*) where the rocks at the entrance to the harbour make it a sheltered anchorage, which became a trading and lime burning centre in medieval times. Later, ships were built, grain exported and lime brought in to be burnt in its ten kilns. In the 19th century, Solva had around 30 registered trading ships some of which certainly handled slate exports. There was one tiny quarry Treflodan SM798263 close at hand, but relatively distant quarries such as Sealyham SM960275 used it in preference to the nearer but much crowded (and expensive) Haverfordwest (*Hwlffordd*). Solva still has a woollen mill one of the only two in a county that once had almost thirty.

Haverfordwest on the Western Cleddau river was the most important town in Pembrokeshire and prior to the development of Milford Haven and Pembroke Dock, the principal port of the county, but its slate significance was slight.

More relevant to slate was the Eastern Cleddau, slate won in its valley being shipped at its limit of navigation at a wharf at Blackpool. As an alternative to Blackpool, St Clears on the Taf offered berthing facilities for larger ships and although it handled little slate after the South Wales Railway came through in the early 1850s, it survived as a steamship port up until the 1930s.

Another anachronistic survival as a river port was Carmarthen where despite having railway connection in 1852, a hundred years later, undeterred by the long and tortuous estuary that had once afforded protection from invaders, steamers were discharging goods onto the section of the A48 that still served as the town quay, barrels and bales forming something of a traffic hazard. There were several slate quarries in the hinterland of the town particularly Llwynpiod SN433299, from where a light railway to Carmarthen (*Caerfyrddin*) was planned, but their markets were local so little slate was shipped here.

Paradoxically of the less than half a dozen slate quarries in Wales to have a standard gauge line running into their quarrying area, two were in Pembrokeshire. In both cases the railway companies involved had been set up primarily to carry slate. In the whole of Wales there is only one other instance of this - the Dinas Mawddwy Railway.

One of the lines was the 1873 Whitland and Taf Railway. Twenty years earlier the Carmarthen & Cardigan Railway had aimed to lay Broad Gauge metal from Carmarthen, through Newcastle Emlyn to a new harbour for Cardigan at St Dogmaels, in view of Brunel's failure to reach Fishguard; the potential would have been enormous. This having failed, the Whitland & Taf was planned to run west from Whitland station, third-railed along the then Broad gauge Great Western (Neé South Wales) Railway before diverging northwest. Since the GWR was converted to Standard gauge before work began, that complication proved unnecessary. Although purporting to reach Cardigan, (which as the Whitland and Cardigan Railway it did almost 20 years later), it terminated at a pub, the Crymmach Arms, not because of any thirst considerations but because it had by then achieved its primary purpose of reaching the Llanfrynach lead mines and more importantly Glogue SN220328 the slate quarry owned by John Owen the line's chief protagonist.

This line consolidated Glogue's position as southwest Wales' largest, most successful and longest lasting (1680s – 1926) slate working. It also with lesser success served neighbouring workings including Pencelli quarry SN192278 that reached it by an incline and Penlan quarry SN207284 that connected to it by a ¾-mile 2'6" horse-drawn tramway. The railway's loading facilities at Llanglydwen also tied in with that singular slate area, the upper Eastern Cleddau.

The slate of the upper Eastern Cleddau was unusual in that, like the English Lake district rock, it was derived not from sedimentary but volcanic material giving it a unique colour and texture. Skilful marketing created a countrywide demand and ensured that at least two or three quarries prospered into the 1930s and beyond. This might have been even more successful had the planned narrow gauge rail link to the GWR been built.

The other line was the Maenclochog Railway built as part of a grand scheme by one Edward Cropper to jointly develop Rosebush and Bellstone slate quarries, SN079300 and SN079302. Starting from near what is now Clynderwen, it too functioned as a standard gauge branch from the GWR, running for just over 8 miles to terminate right alongside the quarry mill. It was a bold and imaginative plan but could not have come at a worse time, the slate market was teetering on the point of collapse and the big north Wales units finding themselves serving shrinking markets turned their attention towards roofing the rows of colliers' housing that were filling the south Wales valleys wall to wall. Since this was the very market that Cropper aimed to serve meant that the project 'Came a cropper'.

The first freight carried by the Maenclochog when it opened in 1876 was indeed slate - a truckload of northern Welsh slates to roof the village flourmill! When it was found that the quarries' output was scarcely filling one train a week, it was decided to re-invent the railway as a tourist carrier, proclaiming the healthful benefits of a bracing (adman's speak for cold and bleak!) environment. The stampede of customers was expected to be so immediate that a temporary hotel was built of corrugated iron to house them until a permanent structure could be built. This latter was never even started and the Rosebush Hotel, the still surviving Tafarn Sinc was, according to a contemporary report merely a place against which cyclists could lean their machines while they ate the sandwiches from their haversacks.

This economically unsuccessful line had a brief revival as the North Pembrokeshire Railway when it was extended to Fishguard in 1895. This extension did pass close, in some cases very close; to slate diggings, but the market had lost its appetite for their marginal product.

The line had a somewhat unusual career during WW1, the track was lifted and sent to France, but was lost when the ship was torpedoed, the upshot being that post-war they received a whole lot of new track by courtesy of the War Office. During WW2 it was commandeered and an inclined section used to provide moving targets for gunnery practise and the tunnel used to try out an idea that the Dambusters 'bouncing bombs' could be bounced into railway tunnels in France to block them in support of the D-Day invasion. It took many attempts before a bomb dropped from a Mosquito aircraft entered the portal of the tunnel. The bomb (unarmed fortunately) bounced successfully along the tunnel, but a 'Back to the drawing board' situation arose when it emerged the other side and bounced for several miles along the track. When the line was derequisitioned it was handed over with the track in better fettle and the banks better trimmed than they had ever been in civilian guise.

The only other railway to have any slate significance was the Central Wales line, whose coming in the 1860s enabled a few trivial workings along its route to at least try to dispose of their products, and encouraged some small but unwise investment.

It must be said that the arrival of the railways was generally bad news for the southwest Wales slate quarries. Particularly away from the coast their customers had little choice but to buy locally, when rail-bourn Bangor and Porthmadog slates began to arrive they had a choice and their choice was not the local product!

Pre-rail, gravestones were made of local slate, its unsuitability for inscribing being often overcome by inserting a plaque of north Wales material for the inscription. Post-rail, gravestones were invariably wholly of north Wales material.

Although road building by slate proprietors in this area was virtually unknown, there was one road that bears comparison with the great slate roads of north Wales such as the Manod and the Gwanas roads. Ystradffin quarry SN787461 built one of the most spectacular quarry roads in Wales. Still in good condition this dizzy corniche is about 1100 yard long rising some 500' to what proved to be a tiny near valueless rogue occurrence of slate.

Since so few diggings were mechanised, foundry and engineering requirements were limited and outside of Cardigan could be taken care of by general blacksmiths and foundries at towns such as Fishguard, Haverfordwest and Carmarthen. There were also merchants and dealers who would have handled slate as an adjunct to other activities, but from the mid 19th century their slate departments would be mainly concerned with distributing north Wales (or imported!) material.

There were certainly no slate settlements on a Blaenau Ffestiniog or Bethesda scale and only the one town Cardigan where slate loomed large. The dispersement of the industry meant that just a few small, dedicated villages arose of which Cilgerran was the most significant where in 1867 it was said of the slate industry *'At first trifling and piddling has become a principal source of employment'*. Better known are the self-contained, self-supporting villages of Porthgain and nearby Abereiddi that had settlements consisting of quarry-owned dwellings. The most ambitious was Rosebush with a terrace of 26 houses that although primitive by present-day standards, were, let at £2 p.a. very much better than any worker in that locality would have hitherto enjoyed. They even had water piped into their homes – fed from the tailrace of the quarry-mill turbine! When post WW2 mains water was supplied, the occupiers complained that it did not taste as clean as the tailrace article!

# 9

# NORTH-EASTERN WALES

Slate in this area was mainly won in four locations, Ceiriog, Llangollen, Corwen and the Tanat valley. None served foreign markets and anyway the distance from the coast ruled out shipment. Fortunately in pre-railway, pre-canal times the existence of roads that were just on the positive side of indifferent, meant that it was possible to deliver to Wrexham, Cheshire and the English Midlands by cart.

Curiously although the Dee, one of Wales' longest rivers flows though the area, the amount of water it carries is insufficient to produce a scour that would enable navigation. Its misleadingly wide valley is not river cut, being either the result of vacation by a larger river (Severn or Mersey?) or to glacial action. At Chester, which in former times was an important port on the Dee, the lack of scour-flow was exacerbated by the overuse of waterwheels and by a weir. In 1737 a five-mile canal was cut to divert the river between Chester and Parkgate on the Wirral, to provide a deeper channel, but this proved inadequate so by the 19th century both passengers and freight for say, Ireland were increasingly going aboard at Parkgate.

It was of course the shortcomings of the Dee that caused traffic to migrate to the Mersey bringing about the rise of Liverpool and Birkenhead.

With the sea being effectively out of reach, the waterborne carriage of slate was, apart from some limited use of the river Severn, confined to the Llangollen and Montgomeryshire offshoots of the Ellesmere canal. Later all the significant workings became dependent on the national rail network, with one standard gauge and three narrow gauge lines being laid down as feeders.

This non-use of coastwise shipping should have given these landlocked workings a competitive advantage during the early years of the 19th century when up to its 1831 repeal, the Slate Tax on coastwise shipments was such a burden on the northwest Wales producers. However, carriage costs still made them uncompetitive with the north Lancashire material creeping coastwise from port to port within the head port of Preston, untaxed.

Slate may have first been commercially worked in this area at Oernant high above the Vale of Llangollen in the 17th century, although this may have well been the source of roofing for Vale Crucis Abbey some 500 years earlier. There were a number of other workings mostly in the Eglwyseg valley, but the two largest diggings Moel Faen SJ185477 and Clogau (Now Berwyn) SJ185463 developed adjacent to Oernant SJ185469 at the head of the Horseshoe Pass to form a significant group. Although the Silurian rock does not always make the best of slates, Moel Faen in particular developed a sound trade in roofing material. Clogau sought to exploit as it still does, the characteristics that make its slate excellent for slab products, unfortunately there was no water on these sites to drive waterwheels to power the saws and planers needed for slab production.

Presumably the adjacent roads to the north and east were used by these quarries for their dispatches. In 1805 the Llangollen extension of the Elsmere canal had been opened to carry limestone from the Eglwyseg scarp, but in order to obtain water from the Dee at Horseshoe Falls it was extended past Llangollen. The opening of the present Horseshoe Pass turnpike in 1811 meant that the canal could be reasonably accessed by the three Oernant workings and in fact Clogau quarry built an incline to join the road just below their quarry.

The problem of sawing was addressed in the 1840s by adapting a flourmill alongside the canal at Pentrefelin SJ218436 as a slate mill, this being an example of the many instances throughout the country of industrialists using their financial muscle to displace corn mills in order to obtain waterpower, a matter of anxiety at a time of rising populations. Although this site had power it lacked the tipping space that a slate mill requires but it was somewhat optimistically assumed that the river could be used, but as on the Teifi at Cilgerran, the fine stuff was carried away to exacerbate silting problems downstream while the off-cuts stayed put causing flooding.

The difficulties of getting slates to the canal and conveying block to the mill were solved in 1852 by the construction of the 3-mile long Oernant Tramway. This was built not to the fashionable 2' gauge, but to 3' to accommodate the large blocks destined for the mill.

Only six years later the railway from Ruabon came through on its way to Bala and Dolgellau and from then on increasing use was made of it, a dedicated siding yard being developed to the east of the mill. This mill, which could also deal with the sawing requirements of other quarries such as Rhiw Goch SJ169453 eventually had 3 circular saws, 8 planers, a sand-polisher and an enamelling oven. Despite protests about river tipping, the slate mill continued in use until the 1920s, being revived in the 1940s by the White Sand and Silica Company to provide ground quartz from sandstone lorried in from Nerquis. This new business supplied the vitreous enamelling market, steel foundries and fine cement trade up to the 1960s, the buildings subsequently being used by the Llangollen Motor Museum.

In the 1860s this mill was supplemented by an on-site steam mill at Clogau, having 4 saws and 2 planers. This mill still functions but now using the most advanced electric machinery.

The tramway was quite a notable construction running from the Clogau quarry (extended to Moel Faen slate quarry in 1857), via short incline to the head of the main incline which had a unique drum house where the brakeman sat in a cabin above the drum to have a clear view down the incline to Abbey Terrace from where it crossed the road at Abbey Dingle to a stone-reverted embankment and viaduct across the Eglwyseg river and on over the canal into the Pentrefelin Slate Works.

A settlement developed at Pentrefelin on the old turnpike road where there were a number of cottages, shops, pubs and two chapels. The cottages at Abbey Terrace also owe their origin to the slate industry and its transport. Near the present Ponderosa café at the top of the pass were Tai-newyddion, a group of houses whose occupants included the men who handled the small, stocky Welsh cobs used both in the quarries and on the upper section of the tramway. These would be taken home overnight, and the first of them to arrive at their respective quarry yards each morning had the job of pulling the trucks that had been loaded the previous afternoon to the top of the incline and to await the arrival of the first up-coming empties. The two ponies that worked between the incline and the works were stabled in the field at the foot of the incline.

The blacksmith (whose forge has now been converted into a private house) tended to live close at hand since he had to begin work early in the morning to see that sharp saw-blades were installed and possibly also stay late at night for the same purpose.

Vying with Oernant for seniority was Craig Rhiwarth SJ053263 quarry at Llangynog in the Tanat valley. It is claimed that it was opened in the 16th century although there seems no positive record before 1797, when it was clearly a long-established working. For a time slate was floated down the Severn to Shrewsbury and Ironbridge, thus being unique in Wales in using a river for inland dispatch (as opposed to using a river to reach the sea), but getting slate (and the nearby lead) to the river was a challenge. Had Telford's Irish Road as was once planned come this way, it would have solved the problem, in the event it was probably well into the 18th century before wagons with teams of horses could conveniently reach the river Severn at Llanymynech, although in the mud and short daylight of winter a carter from Llangynog would often be unable to complete the 30 mile round trip within one day.

Once into the 19th century, the Ellesmere canal that served the Llanymynech limestone workings could be used. Since the English canal network reached almost every English town, this obviously widened the delivery possibilities that hitherto had been effectively confined to the west Midlands, but of course did nothing to shorten the cartage.

From the early 1860s loadings could be made onto the Cambrian Railways at Porth-y-waen, useful but with only a marginally shorter road journey – a traction engine was tried but there was a fearful row with the local council who alleged that it damaged the roads. Undoubtedly true since although a broad-wheeled traction engine would not impose a much greater load on the road surface than a cart, a cart at worst ruts the surface, a traction engine's driving wheels tear it up.

By this time other quarries had opened both in the Llangynog area and in the tributary valley Cwm Maengwynedd, all sharing the same cartage problems, but the other quarries did not have Craig Rhiwarth's difficulties in reaching the carts in the first place. Its workings were high up on a precipitous cliff, finished roofing slate being taken down by sledge to the valley floor some 600' below. The 'driver' seated behind and astride the load could guide the sledge in its presumably very rapid descent, partly by means of a rope and partly by digging in one or other of his heels to provide what we would describe today as 'Differential braking'. The downward journey would not have been the only item in his job description, the other would be to drag the empty sledge back up the near vertical sledge-run, (presumably keeping a sharp look out for the next sledge coming down!). It was the mid 19th century before the construction of the spectacular incline enabled this practice to cease.

Despite the fact that building a railway along the Tanat valley would call for little more than laying track on the ground, there was understandable reluctance to commit capital for restricted revenues. It would benefit the farmers by bringing in fertilisers and other supplies and would have taken out their produce. It could have handled the output of the lead mines but the main freight tonnage would have come from Craig Rhiwarth slate quarry yet its weekly output would have scarcely filled two wagons. There would have been less reluctance to build if the line could have been continued beyond the head of the valley such as was intended by the West Midlands, Shrewsbury & Coast of Wales Railway of 1846, which would have run almost ruler-straight from Worcester and via Llanfair Caereinion, Llanfyllin and Llangynog to Porth Dinllaen (then still being peddled as a port for Ireland), airily ignoring as did railway promoters in those days, of trifling matters such as topography. This GWR-backed scheme was outflanked by the L&NWR's longer but more practicable coast route, which ensured that northern Wales and the Irish traffic would be a L&NWR monopoly. Nevertheless one can stand in Llangynog on a dark night and imagine the Irish Mail explosively bursting through the portals of the tunnel from Llanfyllin, and feel the hammer-beat of a King Class as it passes, its smoke-wreath flooded by the glare of the open fire-box door.

Subsequently the Tanat valley figured in numerous other railway promotions including a further revival of the Porthdinllaen idea that would have gone straight up the Tanat valley. There were several plans to link up with adjacent valleys or to extend existing lines such as the Llanfyllin branch and even a notion that the proposed Llanfair narrow-gauge railway could be diverted to take in Llangynog.

There was coal and limestone in the Llanymynech area and these were well served by branches from the Cambrian's Welshpool to Oswestry line but the lead and slate of the Tanat valley continued to fail to tempt anyone westward. In addition whenever a railway proposal was made public, there would be howls of protest from those that did not want it in their 'Backyards' and equally vociferous cries from those who did. There was broad agreement that a railway was wanted, provided that someone else would be paying for it!

Amongst the crazier ideas was a line, admittedly narrow gauge, up the almost uninhabited Cwm Maengwynedd where the sole mineral was slate in tonnages that would have scarcely filled two trains per year, and unlike the main Tenant valley, there was little prospect of lead.

The arguing went on until the end of the 19th century as to who would put up the capital since realistically there were slim prospects of much if any return on investment. Several factors then came into play that might make a railway a possibility, the Light Railways Act of 1896 reducing the cost both of laying and operating a branch railway, the likelihood of grants from local and central governments and the prospect of granite quarrying to meet the growing demand for road stone. Since Liverpool Corporation's pipe from Lake Efyrnwy crossed the valley at Penybontfawr it had been indicated that a railway up the Tanat valley would be useful for its maintenance; therefore some financial contribution from Liverpool seemed a possibility.

It was only in 1904, when lead mining had ended, slate working was on its last legs and the motor lorry was appearing, that the Tanat Valley Light Railway opened. Operated by and as a branch of, the Cambrian Railways, it was a fairly exiguous affair. Its 15 miles took almost as long to build, as had 118 miles of the GWR's original track from London to Bristol. It was beset by the usual squabbles and cost overruns and in the end by the contractor apparently delaying handover so that he could privately and profitably operate trains on his own account.

Strictly following the easiest route it did pass close to the hamlet of Penybontfawr but Llanrhaeadr-am-mochnant, the only full-blown village in the valley had its station a mile distant, the only station to be close to habitation was the terminus at Llangynog which was of course the only settlement that might be classed as a slate community although it partly owes its existence to lead mining and granite quarrying.

The Craig Rhiwarth incline was extended under a road so that quarry trucks could be run right into the goods yard, making it one of only a handful of slate quarries to have direct access to a main line. The structures were minimal and there is a story that a man sent to collect a henhouse from a station, came back with the waiting room on his cart!

It is interesting that Messrs Maker whose start of granite quarrying at Llangynog was substantially responsible for the survival of the Tanat Valley Railway, was the same firm whose granite dispatches from their workings at Blaenau Ffestiniog was equally useful to the Ffestiniog Railway when its slate tonnages declined.

The Ceiriog valley was also the site of early working, with Tŷ Draw SJ207325 and Craig-y-orin SJ234362 quarries probably supplying roofing to Ruabon, Wrexham and possibly Chester in the 18th century. There were a number of diggings, but only Cambrian SJ189378 Wynne SJ199379 and possibly Nantyr SJ165382 were real commercial operations. Like the Tanat valley workings the opening of the Ellesmere canal enabled slate to be widely distributed but cartage to the canal inflated costs.

It was only when granite began to be worked in the valley on a large scale, did the laying of rails become an economic reality, by which time there was a main-line railway that was nearer to Glyn Ceiriog than the canal. Yet when the Glyn Valley Tramway opened in 1873 it ran to the canal, bridging the railway en-route. This curious ignoring of the railway in favour of the already outmoded canal was due to the fact that the Glyn was being sponsored by the London & North Western Railway who then owned the canal, while the main line in question was Great Western.

The 9-mile Glyn Valley Tramway ran from Glyn Ceiriog towards Chirk before picking up the track bed of a disused colliery line to the canal at Chirk Bank. Other than the ex-colliery section the line was mostly laid alongside the road in the manner of some European light railways. The gauge was the 'Half Standard' 2'4¼" that was the ruling quarry gauge in the area. Passengers were carried but might find themselves riding in empty slate wagons!

Opening as it did just before the slate market collapsed, it was only kept going by the granite business, it being extended to serve the Hendre and other granite quarries and also admitted the defeat of its efforts to deprive the GWR of business and laid a spur to run alongside a siding on the railway.

In 1888 the tramway was diverted and extended as a

steam line to Chirk Station and its adjacent Chirk canal wharf. The revised line did not at first cater for passengers but a passenger (in proper carriages!) and parcels service was restored in 1891. The original locomotives were boxed in and skirted partly for safely (the roadside reservation not being fenced) and allegedly also to avoid frightening the horses. It finally succumbed to road competition in 1935, but Cambrian, its main slate customer soldiered on until manning problems forced closure in 1947.

The fourth slate area in north-eastern Wales was Corwen. It had some old-established slate workings not that far from Llangollen but too far from the end of the canal to be worthy of development, so it was only when the GWR-backed Ruabon – Dolgellau line went through in 1868 could serious quarrying be carried out.

The first major opening was Penarth SJ107424, on the hillside on the southern flank of the valley. Sited directly above the railway a single long incline took wagons down to a siding where adjacent to a water supply, a sawing mill was built. The quarry became quite a substantial working operating on a series of incline-connected terraces, making roofing-slate. Their product proved disappointing and the slate market having collapsed, it closed in 1890. In response to the firming of slate prices, it reopened in 1896 working extensively underground and concentrating almost exclusively on slab products, with sawing being done at the quarry using producer gas.

Just a few miles away was the Deeside quarry SJ138404, whose output reached the main line, via the most singular Deeside Tramway. This 2'7" gauge line was totally anachronistic in having rails of wood sheathed with iron, a construction that had been obsolete for fully a century. This quarry developed in 1869 concentrated on the then burgeoning market for slab, but since there was no power-water on site a fine mill complex, Deeside Slab Works SJ148417 having saws and planers driven by a 30' water wheel was set up ½ mile away. Wagons ran by gravity down to the mill, which also was a headquarters for the combined operation and housed the horses that brought empty wagons back up to the quarry and take finished products along the level section to the head of the incline down to Glyndyfrdwy.

In the early 1870s the tramway was extended (in iron rail) to Moelfferna quarry SJ125399 and at the same time a short extension took it into the Glyndyfrdwy station yard. Eventually with the Deeside quarry closed, reduction was moved from the Deeside Works to an oil-engine driven mill at Moelfferna. Possibly due to the influence of the nearby coalfield, all three tramway inclines and some in the quarry had vertical axis sheaves instead of the near-universal horizontal-axis drum.

Not so successful was the Cletwr quarry SH985348 near Bala. Like the rest it was developed and mechanised to take advantage of the same railway although no rail link to it was ever made.

and finally —

# ANGLESEY

Slate quarrying on Anglesey was on a negligible scale and generally called for neither ships nor trains. At Llanfflewin SH347892 the formations of a quarter-mile tramway to a road were built but never tracked.

However the most imaginative and spectacular 'Materials handling' arrangements in Wales were at Llaneilian SH481932. The procedure probably never fully used, involved lowering product directly into boats from the cliff-top working as was done at several coastal quarries in Cornwall. The difference here was that instead of lowering down the cliff face to a vessel tight against the cliff, material was lowered down a shaft to a ledge cut inside a cave to form a wharf alongside which a ship could lie protected from the elements.

The operation succumbed to the 1870s collapse of slate prices, which since the arrangements included disposing of rubble by tunnels emerging out of the cliff-face; may be thought by some to have been fortunate.

## Quarries directly rail-linked to water or rail

Abereiddi (Tramway to Porth-gain)
Abercorris (Incline, Upper Corris Tramway, Corris Rly to river/rail)
Abercwmeiddaw (Incline, Upper Corris Tramway, Corris Rly to river/rail)
Aberllefenni (Aberllefenni Tramway, Corris Rly to river/rail)
Alexandra (Own railway, North Wales Narrow Gauge to rail)
Arthog (Own tramway to river/rail)
Bellstone/Rosebush (Maenclochog Railway to rail)
Blaen y Cae (Nantlle Railway to sea/rail)
Blaen y Cwm (Rhiw-bach Tramway, Ffestiniog Railway to sea/rail)
Bowydd (Incline to Ffestiniog Railway to sea/rail)
Braich (Robinson tramway to Nantlle Railway, later NWNGR to rail)
Braich Goch (Upper Corris Tramway, Corris Rly to river/rail)
Braich Rhyd (Fron branch North Wales Narrow Gauge to rail)
Bryneglwys (Inclines, Tal-y-llyn Railway to rail)
Brynmawr (Fridd incline to rail)
Bwlch y Groes (Fridd incline to rail)
Bwlch y Slaters (Own branch, Rhiw-bach tramway, Ffestiniog Railway to sea/rail)
Cambrian (Ceiriog) (Incline, Glyn Valley Tramroad to canal/rail)
Cambrian (Cefn Du) (Fridd incline to rail)
Cedryn (Cwm Eigiau Tramway to river)
Cefn Du (Fridd incline to rail)
Cefn y Braich (Croesor Tramway to sea/rail)
Chwarel Fawr (Fridd incline to rail)
Cilgwyn (Inclines, Nantlle Railway to sea/rail, later NWNGR to rail)
Cloddfa'r Coed (Tal-y-sarn sub-branch L&NWR )
Clogau (Oernant Tramway to canal/rail)
Clogwyn y Gwin (North Wales Narrow Gauge Railway to rail)
Conglog (Conglog tramway, Ffestiniog Railway to sea/rail)
Cook & Ddôl (Fridd incline to rail)
Cornwall (Nantlle Railway to sea/rail)
Craig Rhiwarth (Incline, Tanat Valley Railway)
Croesor (Incline, Croesor tramway to sea/rail)
Cwm Ebol (Cwm Ebol tramway to river)
Cwm Eigiau (Cwm Eigiau Tramway to river)

Cwmerau (Ratgoed Tramway, Corris Rly to river/rail)
Cwmorthin (Conglog tramway, Ffestiniog Railway to sea/rail)
Cwt y Bugail (Own branch, Rhiw-bach tramway, Ffestiniog Railway to sea/rail)
Deeside (Deeside Tramway to rail)
Diffwys (Incline, Ffestiniog Railway to sea/rail)
Dinorwig (Dinorwig Railway later Padarn Railway to sea/rail)
Dorothea (Nantlle Railway to sea/rail)
Era/Esgairgeiliog (Own branch, Corris Railway to river/rail)
Fron (Robinson tramway, Nantlle Railway, later NWNGR to rail)
Fron Boeth (Inclines, tunnel, Croesor Tramway to sea/rail)
Fron Goch (Own tramway to river)
Gaewern (Tunnel to Upper Corris Tramway, Corris Rly to river/rail)
Gallt y Fedw (Nantlle Railway to sea/rail)
Gartheiniog (Hendre Ddu Tramway)
Glanrafon (Incline, North Wales Narrow Gauge Rly to rail)
Glogue (Direct to rail)
Glynrhonwy (Upper and lower, Llanberis Branch L&NWR)
Goodmans (Own tramway to rail)
Gorseddau (Gorseddau Rly to sea)
Graig Ddu (Inclines, Ffestiniog & Blaenau Rly, F.R. later GWR/FR to sea/rail)
Hafod y Wern (North Wales Narrow Gauge Rly to rail)
Harlech (Tiny workings may have had tramway to rail)
Hendre Ddu (Hendre Ddu Tramway)
Llechwedd (Incline, Ffestiniog Railway, L&NWR [LMS] to sea/rail)
Llwyngwern (Own tramway, Corris Railway to river/rail)
Maenofferen (Incline,Rhiw-bach tramway, Ffestiniog Railway to sea/rail)
Maes y Gamfa (Hendre Ddu Tramway)
Minllyn (Dinas Mawddwy Railway to rail)
Moel Faen (Oernant tramway to canal/rail)
Moelfferna (Deeside Tramway to rail)
Moeltryfan (North Wales Narrow Gauge Rly to rail)
Moelwyn (Incline to Ffestiniog Railway to sea/rail)
Nant y Fron (Caernarfonshire Slate Quarry Rly, Nantlle Railway to sea/rail)
Nyth y Gigfran (Incline, Ffestiniog Railway to sea/rail)

Oakeley (Incline, Ffestiniog Railway, L&NWR [LMS] to sea/rail)
Oernant (Oernant tramway to canal/rail)
Pant Mawr (Inclines, tunnel, Croesor Tramway to sea/rail)
Parc (Croesor tramway to sea/rail)
Parc Slab (Croesor tramway to sea/rail)
Penarth (Incline to rail)
Pencelli (Incline to rail)
Penlan (Own tramway to rail)
Penrhyn (Penrhyn Railroad, later Penrhyn Railway to sea/rail)
Pen y Bryn (Nantlle Railway to sea/rail)
Penyrorsedd (Nantlle Railway to sea/rail)
Prince of Wales (Gorseddau Junction & Portmadoc Railway to sea)
Ratgoed (Ratgoed Tramway, Corris Railway to river/rail)
Rhiw-bach (Rhiw-bach tramway, Ffestiniog Railway to sea/rail)
Rhosydd (Incline, Croesor Tramway to sea/rail)
Talmeuryn (Hendre Ddu Tramway)
Tal-y-sarn (Nantlle Railway to sea/rail)
Tanrallt (Caernarfonshire Slate Quarry Rly, Nantlle Railway to sea/rail)
Treflan (Incline, North Wales Narrow Gauge Rly to rail)
Tyddyn Agnes (Caernarfonshire Slate Quarry Rly, Nantlle Railway to sea/rail)
Tyddyn Shieffre (Tramway to river/rail)
Tyn y Bryn (Rail direct)
Vaynol (Padarn Railway to sea/rail)
Votty & Bowydd (Incline Ffestiniog Railway to sea/rail)
Wrysgan (Incline to Ffestiniog Railway to sea/rail)
Wynne (Incline, Glyn valley tramway to canal/rail)

**Rigs of Ships**

**Sloop.** Single mast with fore and aft foresail and mainsail on boom, not easy to manage and usually only traded coastally. Smaller examples where usually known as Smacks.

**Ketch.** As a sloop but with a small mizzen mast with spanker sail on a boom. Rarely built in Wales also known as Dandys.

**Brig.** Two masts square rig, the standard Welsh ocean-going craft.

**Snow.** As a Brig but with a small mizzen mast with a boom.

**Ship.** as a Brig but with three masts.

**Brigantine.** Two masts Square rig on foremast, fore and aft on mainmast.

**Barque.** Three masts Square rig on fore and main masts, fore and aft on mizzen (or rarely, four-masted with Square rig on three masts and fore and aft on after mizzen).

**Barquetine.** Three masted, square rig on foremast, fore and aft on main and mizzen masts.

**Schooner.** Two or more masts all with fore & aft sails.

Topsail Schooner. Foremast upper sails square rig lower sails fore and aft, main mast (and mizzen if three-masted) fore and aft rig. These were usually just called schooners and lumped with true schooners were by far the most common type of Welsh rig.

**Flat.** A small Sloop seen on Dee estuary and north Welsh coast.

The assistance of the following is especially acknowledged

Twm Elias
David Gwyn
Bill Jones
Dave Linton
Steffan ab Owain
Martin Riley
Dafydd Roberts
Richard M. Williams

# Abridged bibliography

| | | | |
|---|---|---|---|
| Boyd, J. I. C. | *Tal-y-llyn Railway* | Wild Swan | 1988 |
| Eames, Aled | *Twilight of Welsh Sail* | Univ. of Wales | 1984 |
| Eames, Aled | *Shrouded Quays* | Carreg Gwalch | 1991 |
| Eames, A & Hughes, E. | *Porthmadog Ships* | Carreg Gwalch | 2009 |
| Elis-Williams, M. | *Bangor, Port of Beaumaris* | Gwynedd Arch S | 1988 |
| Freeman, M. | *Aberystwyth* | Ottakar's | 2005 |
| Gale, J. | *The Maenclochog Railway* | Gale | 1992 |
| Gwyn, D. | *Gwynedd, Inheriting a Revolution* | Phillimore | 2006 |
| Holmes, Alan | *Slates from Abergynolwyn* | Gwynedd A S | 1996 |
| Jenkins, J. Geraint | *Maritme Heraitage* | Gomer | 1982 |
| Jenkins, J. Geraint | *Welsh Ships & Sailing men* | Carreg Gwalch | 2008 |
| Kilgour, O. F. G. | *Caernarfonshire Sail* | Carreg Gwalch | 2008 |
| Lewis, M. J. T. | *Sails on the Dwyryd* | Snowdonia N P | 1989 |
| Lewis, W. J. | *The Gateway to Wales* | Dyfed C C | 1990 |
| Lloyd, Lewis | *Sails on the Mawddach* | Lloyd ud | |
| Lloyd, Lewis | *The Brig Susannah* | Lloyd ud | |
| Lloyd, Lewis | *The Unity of Barmouth* | Gwynedd Arch S | 1977 |
| Lloyd, Lewis | *The Port of Caernarfon* | Lloyd | 1989 |
| Lloyd, Lewis | *Pwllheli, Port and Mart of Llŷn* | Lloyd | 1991 |
| Lloyd, Lewis | *Wherever Freights May Offer* | Lloyd | 1993 |
| Lloyd, Lewis | *A real Little Seaport* | Lloyd | 1996 |
| Price, M. R. C. | *The Whitland & Cardigan Railway* | Oakwood | 1976 |
| Rolt, L. T. C. | *Navigable Waterways* | Arrow | 1973 |
| Thomas, D. | *Hen Longau Sir Caernarfon* | Carreg Gwalch | 2007 |
| Williams & Lewis | *Pioneers of Ffestiniog Slate* | Snowdonia N P | 1987 |
| Wilson. E. | *The Ellesmere & Llangollen Canal* | Phillimore | 1975 |
| Wren, W. J. | *The Tanat Valley* | David & Charles | 1968 |

Maritime Wales Various

# Further enjoyable reading on Wales and the Sea

Visit our website for further information:
## www.carreg-gwalch.com

Orders can be placed on our
## On-line Shop